The Young Adult's Guide to Guide to Neuro-Linguistic Programming

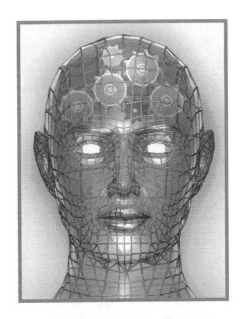

A Step-by-Step Guide to Using NLP to Enhance Your Life

by Melanie Falconer

The Young Adult's Guide to Neuro-Linguistic Programming: A Step-by-Step Guide to Using NLP to Enhance Your Life

Library of Congress Cataloging-in-Publication Data

Names: Falconer, Melanie, author.
Title: The young adult's guide to neuro-linguistic programming : a step by step guide to using NLP to enhance your life / by Melonie Falconer.
Description: Ocala, Florida : Atlantic Publishing Group, Inc., [2017] | Includes bibliographical references and index.
Identifiers: LCCN 2017029530 (print) | LCCN 2017040986 (ebook) | ISBN 9781620231845 (ebook) | ISBN 9781620231838 (alk. paper) | ISBN 1620231832 (alk. paper)
Subjects: LCSH: Neurolinguistic programming.
Classification: LCC BF637.N46 (ebook) | LCC BF637.N46 F35 2017 (print) | DDC 158.1--dc23
LC record available at https://lccn.loc.gov/2017029530

Printed in the United States

PROJECT MANAGER AND EDITOR: Lisa McGinnes • lisa@lisamcginnes.com
COVER DESIGN: Nicole Sturk • nicolejonessturk@gmail.com
INTERIOR LAYOUT AND JACKET DESIGN: Antoinette D'Amore • addesign@videotron.ca

Printed on Recycled Paper

Reduce. Reuse. RECYCLE.

A decade ago, Atlantic Publishing signed the Green Press Initiative. These guidelines promote environmentally friendly practices, such as using recycled stock and vegetable-based inks, avoiding waste, choosing energy-efficient resources, and promoting a no-pulping policy. We now use 100-percent recycled stock on all our books. The results: in one year, switching to post-consumer recycled stock saved 24 mature trees, 5,000 gallons of water, the equivalent of the total energy used for one home in a year, and the equivalent of the greenhouse gases from one car driven for a year.

Over the years, we have adopted a number of dogs from rescues and shelters. First there was Bear and after he passed, Ginger and Scout. Now, we have Kira, another rescue. They have brought immense joy and love not just into our lives, but into the lives of all who met them.

We want you to know a portion of the profits of this book will be donated in Bear, Ginger and Scout's memory to local animal shelters, parks, conservation organizations, and other individuals and nonprofit organizations in need of assistance.

– Douglas & Sherri Brown,
President & Vice-President of Atlantic Publishing

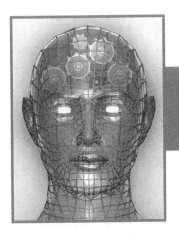

TABLE OF CONTENTS

CHAPTER 7
Metaprograms 121

CHAPTER 8
Anchoring 133

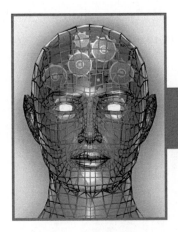

Many of us have felt stuck in patterns that kept us from realizing our goals or are unable to change habits we know hold us back. Neuro-linguistic programming (NLP) offers a way to create new patterns and achieve excellence in virtually every area of your life.

NLP is not a magic wand or cure all; it is a tool. You will only achieve success with NLP if you choose to apply the tools. No special tricks, degrees, or gimmicks are required to achieve success with NLP — it will take practice. As you become more comfortable with the ideas and exercises, you will learn more about yourself and others. You will also feel empowered by your ability to create the changes you want in your life.

NLP combines three distinct components. *Neuro* relates to the brain and the neurological processes involved with sending and receiving information; *linguistic* concerns the verbal and nonverbal information that the brain processes; and finally, *programming* relates to how verbal and nonverbal information sent and received by the brain is interpreted or assigned meaning. In other words, NLP is a fancy name for a combination of processes we do all the time without much thought, such as thinking, seeing, and deciding. NLP gives us the tools to direct these processes in a way that supports our desired outcomes or goals.

How meaning is assigned or information is interpreted depends on individual experiences, values, beliefs, and perceptions. For example, on hearing the words "chair," ten people would likely come up with ten different thoughts and representations. Someone might remember chairing a committee, someone else might imagine a white wooden chair, and someone else might think of a wheel chair or high chair. NLP gives you the tools to manage your own thoughts and perceptions as well as improve your communication skills.

How does NLP do this? It helps you develop useful thoughts and representations as well as respond to the different thoughts and representations of others. When you understand that "chair" can represent many different things, you also understand that the meaning and possibility of any given situation will depend on how you represent the information related to that situation. You will also understand that because "chair" represents different things to different people, you must work to understand the perspective of others in communication.

NLP at its core is about modeling human excellence, according to Grinder and Bandler, the founders of NLP. In other words, it is about copying or emulating someone who has successfully done something you want to do. When you model human excellence, you note which thoughts, behaviors, and resources contribute to success in others and change what you are doing to match what the successful person does. Bandler and Grinder developed NLP to support people in making successful changes in their lives. To make these changes, Grinder and Bandler encouraged people to change what was not working for them and, instead, model patterns that worked for others who had achieved success.

NLP is useful for anyone who wants to achieve excellence at anything from work or sports performance to relationships and personal confidence. Decades of study on the habits of successful people have yielded a body of research that provides information about what successful people do, how they think and frame things, and how they see themselves. People wanting to achieve success can duplicate that success by applying the same strategies in their own lives.

Much like the blueprints for building a house, NLP provides the guide for taking a vision or a plan from thought to being. Achieving excellence with NLP involves creating change through deliberate integration of minds (both conscious and subconscious or unconscious), language, and behavior. In the simplest terms: as you think, you are. That does not mean becoming a star athlete is simply a matter of visualizing yourself winning a gold medal. It does mean that because we determine what the information we receive means, we can actively work to change meaning, thus changing results and our lives in the process.

The following are some tips for getting the most from your experience with this book:

- Refer to the definitions and concepts in the quick-start guide as you read the book and complete the exercises until you are comfortable with each of them.

- Make notes of any goals you want to accomplish. Use the tools in this book to help you form and accomplish your goals.

- Practice each of the ideas and exercises. Keep a journal as you move through the book to chart your progress. You might also consider going through the book with a friend who will hold you accountable for the goals you set and celebrate with you as you accomplish each of them.

- Give particular attention to the case studies included throughout the book. These studies give useful examples from NLP practitioners for achieving results with NLP.

- Be patient with yourself as you work through this book. Remember, your attitude will shape your experience.

With an open mind and a pen ready, enjoy!

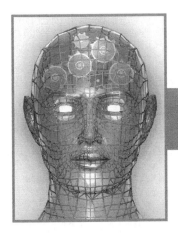

CHAPTER 1

What are the Guiding Principles of Neuro-Linguistic Programming?

Whdt is NLP? What are its guiding principles? What legitimate questions! Chances are, even if you are a high school student who has taken a class in Psychology, you will not know what NLP is.

In simple terms, neuro-linguistic programming allows us to reframe our subconscious beliefs that may be holding us back. It is a set of tools that allow us to free ourselves of our limitations. Using these tools, we can take unconscious beliefs or patterns of behavior, unlearn them, and replace them with healthier ones.

In other words, if there's something you want in life, be it a position in student government, a part in a play, or simply a better attitude, NLP shows us how to produce a desired change or outcome.

Many people carry unhealthy habits with them into adulthood. Were you a whiner when you were a child but still whine as a young adult? It makes sense that whining got you what you wanted or needed when you were a child, but trust me: your boss will never give you a raise if you whine for it. Chances are, you'll be fired. Maybe you learned to be passive aggressive, using withdrawal and guilt to manipulate your parents, relatives, or friends to get what you want. This won't get you anywhere with your teachers, employers, teammates, or anywhere in life, period.

Whatever unhealthy habits you learned as a child, this is the time to unlearn them and learn about the *art of success* using NLP. This first chapter will serve as an introduction to the basic principles (referred to as "presuppositions") and their relevance to your life to get you started.

The Basic Concepts of NLP

Commonly referred to as "concepts," these are perhaps better referred to as the six steps to getting what you want. Think about them like the tools and materials you need to construct a ship to weather a fierce storm. The first steps involve knowing your destination: what you want out of life, what you want to achieve, and imagining this to its fullest extent. The following ones are about weathering the turbulent seas to get there.

Take a minute to engage with these concepts and use a journal as an aid:

1. Think in terms of what you want; avoid thinking about what you do not want.

2. Create a clear mental picture of what you want;
   see what you want.
3. Feel yourself experiencing what you want.
   Make the experience as vividly real as you can;
   this will become easier with practice.
4. Determine if you have the resources needed to
   get what you want.
5. Choose to be accountable for what you can control.
6. Anticipate and plan for any obstacles.

Presuppositions of NLP

Neuro-linguistic programming is based on a number of tenets that allow us to train our minds to achieve excellence.

If your mind is like a domesticated lion, brimming with potential but estranged from its natural might, think of these as the steps to re-teach your mind its natural way. If you're found consistently dwelling on your problems in your room on a Saturday night, if you're always preoccupied with your own thoughts, these will teach you to re-frame the struggles in your life so that you can meet your desired outcome.

The map is not the territory

Each of us has made a "map" of life. We've looked around a bit, seen some things, and boom! We make a generalized map based off of what we see. This map is often full of generalized assumptions. For instance, maybe you tried out for ten plays and didn't get into a single one. Maybe you've included "I'm a failure" in your personal map based off of your experience.

These maps become software programs that govern what you think, say, and do. The map can only be a partial representation of the actual possible territory, which is vast. In other words, one person's map can never fully express what the entire world actually is. The map can only express information that has been filtered through your perceptions over time.

Think of a modified game of Scrabble as another example. Four players get the same seven letters, making more than one hundred words possible. One player might see 20 different word possibilities that can be spelled using the letters. Another might see only one word, another might see 55, and the last player may not be able to find any words among the letters at all. As players gain more skill and knowledge, they will be able to see more possible words among the letters. Until they gain more skill and knowledge, the number of possible words they see will be limited.

In other words, we need to expand your map to take account of all of the possibilities. They are, indeed, endless.

People respond based on their individual map

We each have our own map. This map is drawn as we collect information through our senses and made up of the conclusions we draw from them. Much of that information settles in our subconscious mind without our conscious awareness.

Even though everyone has their own different map, the true reality of the world is the same. Think back to our Scrabble game. Just because you do not see the word possibilities does not mean they do not exist. Our maps are different because our perceptions are different.

An Indian fable represents this concept well: there are several blind men whose task it is to describe an elephant before them. One feels its nose. The other feels its tusk. The other its feet, so on and so forth. When they come together to try and describe the beast, they are at a loss, fiercely defending their own perception.

You don't have to fight for your perception of the world, your map, or *should* fight for it. You should accept that your map is as narrow as the person's sitting next to you, and open your eyes to a broader truth: the territory.

This understanding brings an awareness that a wide array of responses are possible in a given situation. If you feel you're not finding success in the world, don't fight with the arrogance of the men trying to fight for their narrow perception of the elephant. Widen your point of view, and then hone in on a map that works for you. We can change the world, as we experience it, by changing our maps.

There is no failure — only feedback

When you attempt to do something and you don't get what you want or expected, it is useful to view the experience as one you can learn from rather than one that was wasted or failed. Maybe you tried making a new friend and you acted aggressively towards them. Maybe your audition for the school play tanked miserably and you'll have to wait until next year to try out for the musical. These rejections hurt, and they do unfortunately shape a huge portion of our young adult life. They can still be a potential resource to you, however, if you choose to learn from them.

Take a look at the following list of "failures" and see how they can be learning experiences.

Failures or Feedback?

1831: Lost job

1832: Lost bid for Illinois State Legislature

1833: Lost a business

1835: Lost a sweetheart

1836: Suffered a nervous breakdown

1838: Lost a bid for Illinois House Speaker

1843: Lost a bid for nomination to U.S. Congress

1849: Not chosen for land officer job

1854: Lost bid for the Senate

1856: Lost bid to become U.S. Vice President

1858: Lost another bid for the Senate

Now at the year 1858, wouldn't you guess that this guy would just give up already? Well, he didn't and you should be glad because if he did, our country would be an entirely different place than it is today. This list of "failures" belongs to Abraham Lincoln, elected 16th president of the United States in 1860. Imagine if he had allowed himself to become paralyzed or stagnant each time he did not accomplish his desired outcome. When considering your own so-called failures, it is important to do as Lincoln did and keep moving toward the desired outcome.

Evaluating and learning from feedback rather than stamping these losses as "failures" fosters feelings of agency. Agency is a sense of control and motivation towards an end goal. So rather than saying, "I will never be able to get a spot on the water polo team because I'm not in shape at all," you can review and rework past plans. For example, maybe you had a great exercise plan, but you got preoccupied hanging out with friends or caught a cold and lost momentum. Using that feedback, you might rework your plan by telling your friends you'll be unavailable the next couple of days, taking some Vitamin C supplements, and re-working an exercise regime that works for you.

With a journal and notebook in hand, think of a recent "failure." What is it you can learn from it? What about the rejection is within your control? Was it simply not in your control? What will you do better next time?

The meaning of communication is the response it gets

Nag, nag, nag, nag.

Isn't this what you hear when your mom doles out a pitchy scream from the kitchen, reminding you to do your homework, clean your room, and take the trash out? It's almost like they've invented a special language designed to get on your nerves. (Maybe next time try saying, "Sorry, I don't speak Nag.")

The fact is parents usually intend to communicate love and concern. What teens often hear is angry, frustrated badgering, and of course, they respond in kind. The original message — such as *I care about what happens to you and I want you to be a responsible human being* — is lost amidst angry feelings.

If it seems you are constantly misunderstood or listener responses demonstrate that they took away a meaning you did not intend, it is *you* who can improve. If someone is consistently not understanding you, you can take responsibility for the miscommunication and take action to clarify your meaning. The bonus? Better relationships.

If what you are doing is not working, do something different

I like to call this step: "Avoid falling into the pits of insanity."

It may sound ingenuine or dramatic, but it is a mistake that so-called "normal" people are guilty of every single day. They do the same thing, get the same results, and are constantly disappointed. Do they change what they are doing? Frequently, they don't. This is the definition of insanity.

If we're being honest, most of us can find multiple examples of things we do that we know do not work but do them anyway. You wait until the last minute to do your midterm paper; you put off practicing a routine and don't perform as well as you know you could; or you spend your allowance on chocolate bars instead of saving up for a summer trip. The examples of how we all continue to do things that do not work are endless. Most of us have at least one place where we would benefit greatly by doing something different. No matter how long you have had a habit or behavior, it is not permanent.

Shocking?

Simply recognizing this fact can open you to the possibility that you *can* do something different. Behavior can be changed. Dr. Sandra Chapman, founder of the Center for Brain Health at The University of Texas at Dallas, believes the brain is among the most modifiable parts of the human body. We know from scientific research that adult brains are, indeed, malleable. Like child brains, adult and young adult brains are also capable of generating change and new cells. This phenomenon, called neuroplasticity, means that new experiences can change our neurons — the nerve cells in the brain — and how they are organized.

What does that mean for you? No matter how long you have had a habit, even if it has been decades, the brain can adapt and develop new patterns for new habits.

You cannot not communicate

Communication is more than what you say; it is both verbal *and* nonverbal. You are almost always communicating without even knowing it.

You may even be communicating when you decide to sit in some far off corner of the room, wanting anything *but* communication.

Freaky, right?

Everything about you, from your clothes to your body language, communicates a message. We all use language, facial expressions, and body cues that reveal something about the way we think and feel. In numerous academic studies, it was found that 93 percent of communication involved nonverbal cues such as body language and tone of voice. The remaining seven percent involved what we actually say.[1]

When it comes to communication, one of the goals is **congruence.** Congruence happens when your subconscious and conscious mind are aligned. That alignment helps you present a consistent message because what you say matches what you do, how you present yourself, and what kind of nonverbal cues you're initiating. You are said to be incongruent when what you say does not match the other things you're communicating.

---

[1]**http://ubiquity.acm.org/article.cfm?id=2043156**

Needless to say, incongruence is not how you want to operate.

Here's an all too common example. You might say you are interested in what a person is saying, but you're checking text messages, catching a glance at yourself in the mirror, or letting your mind wander while he or she is talking. Your words indicate one message: "I am interested in what you are saying," but your behavior communicates a different message: "I have more interesting or important things to do than listen to what you are saying."

So, check yourself. Make yourself pay attention. Or else, ask them to change the topic or admit you're spaced out.

Individuals have all the resources they need to achieve their desired outcomes

Everyone has the power to create change in his or her own life. A rather comforting expression validates this,:"Even a broken clock is right twice each day." Everyone, no matter the circumstance, has a strong and perfect place from which to build. This presupposition allows you to change your interpretation of some behaviors and reconsider others. For example, suppose you have tried to lose weight in the past without success. The problem is not the goal or your ability to accomplish it; it is your willingness to understand how to direct your internal resources toward accomplishing the goal.

Underlying every behavior is a positive intent

The presupposition that underlying every behavior is a positive intent is not a license to commit or reason to promote bad behavior. Examples of bad behavior include bullying, hitting, yelling, stealing, and lying.

Instead of using this statement as a justification for cruelty, first consider the legendary English hero Robin Hood who is said to have robbed from the rich (negative behavior) to give to the poor (positive intent). When we uncover the underlying positive intention behind "bad" behavior — wanting justice for the poor — we can look for and adopt new behaviors that more closely match the intention. In our own lives, this would mean looking for the reward or payoff we get for bad behavior. We must then look for positive ways to get the same or a better payoff so that our behavior change is supported.

People are much more than their behavior

This presupposition follows organically from the previous. It involves separating behavior and intention.

Most of us have heard about separating the deed from the doer. Individuals are quite complex and cannot be fully understood just by what they do. Think of a student with above-average intelligence who consistently underperforms. You know they're smart. You know they could do better. This is what we have to look at: we are more than what we do because the possibilities for what we can do are limitless.

Behavior is or can be always changing. It is not fixed. That's what you have to understand when interacting with others, and when dealing with yourself: we all have the capacity to match our behavior to our potential. The more we do this, the more we grow into the person we were born to be.

People make the best choices available to them

We may wonder how people end up in jail, in jobs they hate, or with addictions. Each of us makes choices based on our own individual history, values, beliefs, and experiences. We do the best we can with what we believe is available to us. We bring our own unique worldview and perception to each decision we make.

In some cases, our worldview obscures the full range of possibilities, leaving us to select from limited choices. When we remember that the map is not the territory, we understand that we can broaden our worldview or rework our maps to add more choices. Remember that even when you do not see a choice, there likely is one there that will become visible with a different map or a different perspective.

The key here is to look at the territory. You may *think* you can only go in a certain direction (try drugs, slack off, etc.) but it's at this moment you should think about *all* the choices available. This is the time to re-evaluate your map and chose differently.

Consider this take on perspective around priorities.

CASE STUDY: Big Rocks

Name: Dr. Christina Puchalski
Title: Internist and Geriatrician
District: Washington D.C.

At a workshop on setting priorities, the facilitator asked each participant to talk a little about what she or he hoped to gain during the next two hours.

Many people talked about feeling overwhelmed, stressed, and like they were running in place. No matter how busy they were or how fast they ran they just could not seem to do the things that really needed to be done. There just do not seem to be enough hours in the day, several people lamented.

Overwhelmingly, those present in the room were seeking ideas and support for achieving work-life balance. They wanted to know the magic formula for "doing it all."

Much of what was discussed that afternoon was based on Stephen Covey's *Seven Habits of Highly Effective People*. The focus was on two habits specifically: "Put first things first" and "Begin with the end in mind."

Using those habits as a springboard, participants spent a good bit of time crafting the beginnings of a personal mission statement. Like the mission statements created in boardrooms or for business plans, personal mission statements can help clarify, direct, and motivate. These statements can also help us prioritize or identify what Covey calls our "Big Rocks" (those things that are most important to you, such as your relationship with your relatives, friends, teachers, or time spent on things you love).

When we begin to distinguish our big rocks from the little rocks in our lives, it becomes easier to order our priorities accordingly. Little rocks are the things that might be important but might not move us closer to our life purpose or goals. They might not be important for any reason other than to keep us busy or protect us from the discomfort of saying "no" if we are not good at setting boundaries. To illustrate this point, the facilitator showed a clip from a Covey workshop.

In the clip, an audience member comes to the stage. She is presented with a bucket nearly full of little rocks. Several big rocks sat on the table beside the bucket and beside that was an empty bucket.

Her challenge: Get all the rocks in one bucket. She tried hard. The woman pushed little rocks this way and that, she shifted and turned the big rocks, she puzzled and persevered, but she could not make them all fit in the bucket.

After many diligent attempts, the solution came to her. She put each of the big rocks in the empty bucket, and then she arranged the little rocks to fit around the big rocks.

With this in mind, what would you say are the little rocks in your life? Is this too much time on the computer? Too much time spent with friends you don't even really like? Too much time lazing around?

Now what are the big rocks? How can you make time for these in your daily life?

Modeling successful performance leads to excellence

Modeling successful performance shows that if one person can do something, anyone can learn to do it. Unlike more traditional therapy, which is highly recommended to those who may need it, NLP is not concerned with describing the problems we experience or uncovering why we have problems.

Let's say you have to present in front of your class and you have enormous stage fright. With NLP, you would not focus on *why* you are paralyzed by stage fright. NLP deals with the moment to moment: the facial expressions you see when you're in front of your classmates, how you interpret them, and how to change your interpretation.

When someone experiences success, we can duplicate that success by understanding how his or her thoughts, actions, and feelings came together to produce that success. We can then apply those patterns in our own lives. If you notice that a confident classmate is completely focused on their subject matter, and holds themselves upright, take note of this behavior. Try and take note of this for yourself so you can emulate it in your next presentation.

It may be difficult at first, but the saying "fake it 'till you make it" is a relevant one. Think of excellence like a new super-suit: you may not feel comfortable, but give it a while, and you'll be walking around like nothing can touch you!

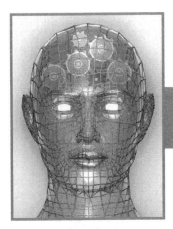

CHAPTER 2

NLP Key Terms and Foundations

Now that we've covered all of the presuppositions of NLP, we can move onto the basic terms that will be used in the remaining discussions of the book. Just as you've been writing down notes (because we know you have!), try to write these down for your reference somewhere, highlight them, or put a tab in these pages to reference later on.

The Four Learning Levels of NLP

Learning a new skill generally happens in four phases or levels of competence. The levels take the learner from beginner to expert as knowledge and confidence grows. The four levels of learning are called subconscious incompetence, conscious incompetence, conscious competence, and subconscious competence. An explanation of each follows.

Subconscious incompetence

At the subconscious incompetence level, the learner not only does not have the skill, the learner is not even aware of his or her skill deficit. Maybe you think you're really great at winning people over, but what if half of your classmates feel like they can only tolerate you? This is an example of subconscious incompetence: you *think* you're good at something but you're not.

Conscious incompetence

At the conscious incompetence level, the learner begins to understand that the skill deficit exists, but does not yet have command of the skill. Now you understand that smacking your gum loudly is driving everyone else nuts. Maybe you talk too loudly, an observation gleaned from the other students "itching" their ears every time you speak. Now you're aware of the problem, but have yet to fix it.

Conscious competence

At the conscious competence level, the learner is developing the skill. You've lowered your voice. You don't bring gum to school. People are starting to give your high fives: you're liked and you know it!

Subconscious competence

Finally, at the subconscious competence level, the learner has fully mastered the skill. You don't have to think twice about it, just like riding a bike.

Let us use a student who has bad communication skills: the one who comes off as aggressive without really intending harm onto others. At the beginning level of subconscious incompetence, they don't understand that his or her communication style is off-putting. He or she cannot figure out why their fellow peers seem to be on the verge of splashing them with holy water, turning their heads away and avoiding eye contact during class discussions. The student is found scratching their head: what did they say to deserve such icy shoulders?

Wanting to improve, the student may ask for feedback from their teachers or peers. In taking this step, they've reached conscious incompetence. He or she is aware that his or her communication style is at the root of the problem, but does not yet have the skills to improve the style.

Now they move onto the next evolution: conscious competence. He or she uses feedback information to practice communication strategies that build rapport with others and reduce resistance. The skills are emerging and not yet automatic or "second nature" because our learner is consciously working to develop new communication skills.

With time, the student arrives at their final destination: subconscious competence. He or she uses new verbal and nonverbal cues to create connections with their teachers and peers. The new skill has become a habit that is patterned in his or her brain. Students are more receptive to what they have to say because now instead of looking to the floor and communications ideas vehemently, they've opened up their face to the classroom and even smile now and again! Better yet? This all comes to them naturally now. Subconscious competence indicates mastery of a skill. Our learner can now use the new skills without conscious thought, or subconsciously, because they are "second nature."

Representation

Representation refers to the mental picture you create upon hearing a cue. What comes to mind when you hear the adjective "mean," "kind," or "likeable?" Each person will form a different picture. This seems obvious: everyone has different definitions for what they like or don't like, or what they consider particularly negative. What you don't know: your representation of things can have a positive or negative effect on your relationships and achievements.

Pillars

The pillars, or building blocks, of NLP are the following:

- Rapport
- Outcome thinking
- Sensory awareness
- Behavioral flexibility

These pillars are basically skills that will help you master all the presuppositions of NLP. They are almost like "prerequisites:" things you have to master before you embark on mastering the art of NLP. *A discussion of these pillars is included in Chapter 4.*

Framing

Framing concerns your perceptions of an event or circumstance and the choices you think are available to you based on those perceptions. In simpler terms, your attitude — how you think and talk about something — has a direct impact on how you feel about it and what you think you can do about it. Our framing is also based on our personal maps. We may have a certain attitude towards something because of the ways we've limited ourselves.

State

The term state is used to describe, in total, the emotions, thoughts, and feelings you are experiencing in the moment. In other words, the state you are in describes what is going on with and for you internally. For example, you may be in a calm or agitated state. NLP teaches you to achieve your desired outcomes by *"breaking state,"* more specifically a state that is dysfunctional. *Breaking state, which refers to moving from your current emotional state into another one, most often from a negative or non-productive place to a more useful one, will be described in Chapter 8.*

Metaprograms

Metaprograms determine our patterns of interaction during communication. In other words, your metaprogram will govern your verbal and nonverbal communication habits. When you change metaprograms, you will notice that your communication patterns change as well. Metaprograms also determine what strategies we will choose to get anything done and whether we act on a *toward-* or *away-from motivation.*

When you take action because you want to *avoid* something — such as being embarrassed in front of other people your age or unprepared for school — you are using an *away-from* motivation. Using an away-from motivation means you are motivated to avoid an outcome by completing the action. People that are motivated in this way take action to avoid the thing they do not want to happen. When you take an action, such as signing up for tryouts or trying out a new personal hobby, you are using a toward motivation. Using a toward motivation means you are motivated by the outcome or reward you will get on completing the action. People using a toward motivation take action to experience something they want to happen.

Basically, a more successful metaprogram would use a "toward motivation" because conversations would be solution-based. Metaprograms inspired "away-from motivations" are usually based on fear, which anyone can smell from a mile away. The book will go into more detail on how to construct positive metaprograms for communicating later on.

Anchoring

Remember the exercise in the previous section? An anchor grounds us in the best state for achieving our goals: it's a physical reminder associated with a memory of confidence and joy. It is a signal or reminder to assume a posture or attitude for success. Yet anchors can also be set up unintentionally or trigger an unwanted state. Maybe you have something called "misophonia," defined as a deep hatred of human-made sounds such as chewing, breathing loudly, or shuffling papers (something I personally used to suffer from). These sounds make you incredibly angry; they are anchors for a negative state. When this happens, you can learn to change your response by extinguishing the anchor. *This will be discussed further in Chapter 8.*

History of NLP

At this point, we hope you've garnered enough interest in NLP to read about how it was founded. The founders are John Grinder and Richard Bandler and they both share credit for creating neuro-linguistic programming. They based NLP on language patterns used by Frederick (Fritz) Perls and Laura Perls, founders of Gestalt therapy; Virginia Satir, considered to be the mother of family therapy; Gregory Bateson, a philosopher; and Milton Erickson, a psychiatrist and renowned hypnotherapist.

Richard Bandler holds both a Bachelor of Arts and Master of Arts in psychology. It was research on therapists such as Gestalt and Satir that inspired Bandler, who was initially devoted to matters of mathematics, to pursue degrees in psychology. If you ever get the chance to search through his history on the internet, there's no doubt you'll find some controversial rumors and stories about the man. Most of them arise from his period of heavy drug addiction and murder charges. Of course this doesn't paint him in the greatest light: just keep in mind we're all multifaceted human beings and even (if not especially) our greatest thinkers are host to some controversial secrets.

Grinder, the less controversial of the pair, was born in 1940 and holds a bachelor of arts in psychology and a Ph.D. in linguistics.

Bandler and Grinder met at the University of California at Santa Cruz (UCSC) where they led weekly Gestalt therapy groups in the mid-1970s for UCSC students. Gestalt therapy helps people separate thoughts and feelings that are caused by what is happening in the present moment from those that are left over from the past. According to Gary Yontef, Ph.D., in his book *Awareness, Dialogue and Process,* Gestalt therapy focuses more on process (what is happening) than content (what is being discussed). With Gestalt therapy, the emphasis is on what is being done, thought, and felt at the moment rather than on what was, might be, could be, or should be.

Initial Gestalt therapy groups emulated founder Fritz Perls as closely as possible, from his accent and communication style to his habit of smoking. Bandler and Grinder used their theory of modeling human excellence with the goal of isolating the behaviors that led to Perls' success. Identifying and isolating behaviors helped them both understand which ones should be kept and which ones could be discarded (such as the smoking).

Grinder and Bandler duplicated this process with other therapists, such as Virginia Satir. Satir, a founder of family therapy and instrumental in the creation of the first family therapy program in the United States, believed that family and therapeutic relationships would be more successful when they emphasized love, nurturing, and warmth. Satir thought many people hold onto beliefs that served them at one time — such as when they were children — but later held them back. She taught people how to move beyond beliefs that were not useful to create deeper and richer life experiences.

From this research, Grinder and Bandler learned many things that would become the foundation of neuro-linguistic programming. For example, they noticed that the successful therapists used similar linguistic patterns. Linguistic or language patterns include things such as speech, grammar, sentence structure, and word phrasing. They also noticed that the therapists responded to clients using the client's representational system. For example, if the client used a visual representational system, the therapist might use responses such as, "*It is clear to me*" or "*I see what you mean.*" Bandler's master's thesis, which was eventually published in 1975 as volume one of *The Structure of Magic,* is based on findings from these research groups. A follow-up, *The Structure of Magic, Vol. 2,* was published the following year.

Grinder and Bandler expounded on their early work by studying Milton Erickson. As a young man, Erickson was diagnosed with polio. He spent more than a year in an iron lung — a respirator that encloses the entire body, except the head, and helps with breathing. After his time in the chamber, still bedridden, Erickson watched family and friends closely. Through sharp observation, he taught himself to interpret and understand the conscious and unconscious ways people behave and relate. Erickson would later use his observations to revolutionize the fields of psychotherapy and hypnosis. Bandler and Grinder used Erickson's work to teach people how to understand and duplicate excellence in their own lives.

This is their goal that they wish to achieve with NLP: to get rid of undesirable behaviors to make room for successful ones. With NLP, the problem is not the person; people work perfectly. The problem is the pattern of behaviors that result from our thinking and feeling. Our job in modeling human excellence is to learn what patterns successful people use and employ them in our own lives. This is what the foundations of NLP were based on and what the founders want to continue to foster in their work.

The Growth of NLP

NLP was a new idea in the 1970s. Today, it is the subject of hundreds of seminars, articles, CDs, DVDs, and books. Some of the best known of these books include Tony Robbins' *Unlimited Power: The Science of Personal Achievement, Change Your Mind and Keep The Change,* and *Frogs Into Princes,* transcripts of Bandler and Grinder's seminars edited by Steve and Connirae Andreas. There are also dozens of NLP training centers located around the world. Researchers and practitioners continue to discover new applications and strategies in the quest for excellence. Although NLP has encountered some skepticism in mainstream psychology, many real life examples of change have been documented by researchers and practitioners alike. This book is written in the hope that you too will find what you need to create the changes you want in your life.

Criticism of NLP

Though the number of proponents has grown since its development by Bandler and Grinder, NLP is not without detractors. NLP has not enjoyed the same mainstream acceptance as other disciplines such as psychotherapy. This is, in part, owed to the fact that NLP has not been largely embraced by academicians providing the type of in-depth research that leads to their stamp of approval. Wider acceptance of NLP has also been hampered by what can only be called a fringe element.

NLP offers very accessible concepts and ideas, such as using rapport to influence behavior, which a few people have taken and misused. As a result, some people hold the mistaken impression that NLP is about wild mind tricks designed to take advantage of people and part them from their money. This could be true for some people who wish to use NLP as a tool to wield power over someone else, but the careful reader should be reminded that there is opportunity for abuse in any field. The greater opportunity that exists, and that we hope you seize upon, is the opportunity to grow and learn more about yourself.

CASE STUDY:
Successful use of NLP

Judith E. Pearson, Ph.D.
Motivational Strategies, Inc.
Licensed professional counselor
judy@engagethepower.com

I took my first practitioner training in 1988 and have been practicing NLP since then. I have practitioner, master practitioner, and trainer certifications in NLP, with over 17 years of teaching NLP and over 20 years of using it in my practice as a licensed professional counselor. I teach for various organizations around the Washington, D.C. area, such as the American Hypnosis Training Academy and Ultimate Success Coaching. I have also written around 100 book reviews on NLP and hypnosis since 1997.

I use NLP principles in my practice and in teaching NLP as a practical guide to understanding human behavior, explaining what I do, and in my choice of NLP interventions. I conduct individual therapy and coaching mostly with adults and occasionally with adolescents. I work with behavioral, emotional, health, and performance issues.

In terms of who can benefit from NLP, I think anyone over the age of five with average, or better, intelligence can benefit from some aspect of NLP. In fact, most people can learn NLP principles on their own. People usually can benefit from the skills of a practitioner by learning the patterns, strategies, and communication skills. NLP provides a framework for many different approaches to behavioral change, and each practitioner can adapt NLP to his or her own style and the needs of his or her clientele.

Each NLP session is unique because I use it to address a wide range of issues. I often combine various forms of hypnosis with NLP. Usually, my sessions include a well-formed outcome and an NLP pattern to help the client access resources or new decisions, understandings, or strategies regarding the problem at hand.

I remain very formal with the patterns, although I might add my own variations. I think the intuitive part comes about from empathy and rapport — an unconscious connection between myself and the client that tells me what to say when.

Although many people make a distinction between NLP and hypno-therapy, I do not see much difference between them. I purposely use trance work in NLP. However, because most lay people are not familiar with the benefits of NLP, I advertise my services as a hypnotherapist. Therefore, many of my clients have the expectation that they will get to experience what one client referred to a "real hypnosis," in which they simply lean back, close their eyes, and let me do most of the talking. For these sessions, I take the more traditional approach, with a formal trance induction, deepening, and directing suggestions. I might also add in guided imagery, mental rehearsal, reframing, and NLP patterns.

I think the most important benefit of NLP is that it is experiential for clients: They participate in the process through visualization, revivifica-tion of memories, accessing internal resources, following new strate-gies, and mental rehearsal. They actually get to experience the changes taking place throughout the session. A common denominator for what people are looking for is help to do the one thing they want to do, but do not or cannot bring themselves to do.

NLP is so ingrained in my thinking that I use it automatically, without planning or conscious awareness that I am doing it. NLP has given me a solution-orientation to every challenge I face. NLP has also become the way I earn my living and has significantly improved my interperson-al skills.

I follow the NLP model to build and use rapport, which means matching and mirroring, pacing and leading, and communicating empathically. I also believe anchoring is critical to the NLP process. Anchoring helps the client access a resourceful state in which he or she can then imple-ment solutions to the presented problem. This matters because people cannot solve a problem within the parameters of the problem. They have to do something different that they have not experienced before.

I use both the meta model and the Milton model because each serves a purpose in the context of counseling and coaching. The meta model is useful for gathering information and often for inviting the client to think about the problem in a new way. I use the Milton model when doing trance work or when I want the client to respond in a unique way as a result of transderivational search, such as when I want clients to arrive at their own interpretations and meanings of what I say.

I do not agree that NLP is not supported by science. NLP has been subjected to some experimental studies and found to be effective. Moreover, NLP incorporates elements of methods and approaches that have been shown in experimental studies to be highly effective in behavioral change including rapport, empathy, imagery, trance work, and mental rehearsal.

With NLP, I have success nearly every day that I am in sessions with my clients. Recently, I worked with a highly depressed client. She was off work on disability leave for depression and recently returned to her job. Her interpersonal communication skills with coworkers were not as good as they could have been, which was a continuing problem for her, and she had low self-esteem. I helped her mentally rehearse how to relate to coworkers from a resourceful state. At one point she said, "I'm always afraid I'll fail — no matter what I do."

I rejoined with the NLP principle that all failure is feedback containing useful information, and it says nothing about her worth as a person. This was a conversational reframe. I continued talking, but apparently, she heard nothing I said after that. She became very silent and just stared at me. When I stopped talking she said, "I just realized something. I am not the sum total of all my failures." She said this with great exuberance and repeated it. It was a life-changing moment for her. This client said to me on our third session, "I've spent three years in cognitive therapy learning how broken I was, and in three sessions with you, I've got a whole new outlook on life."

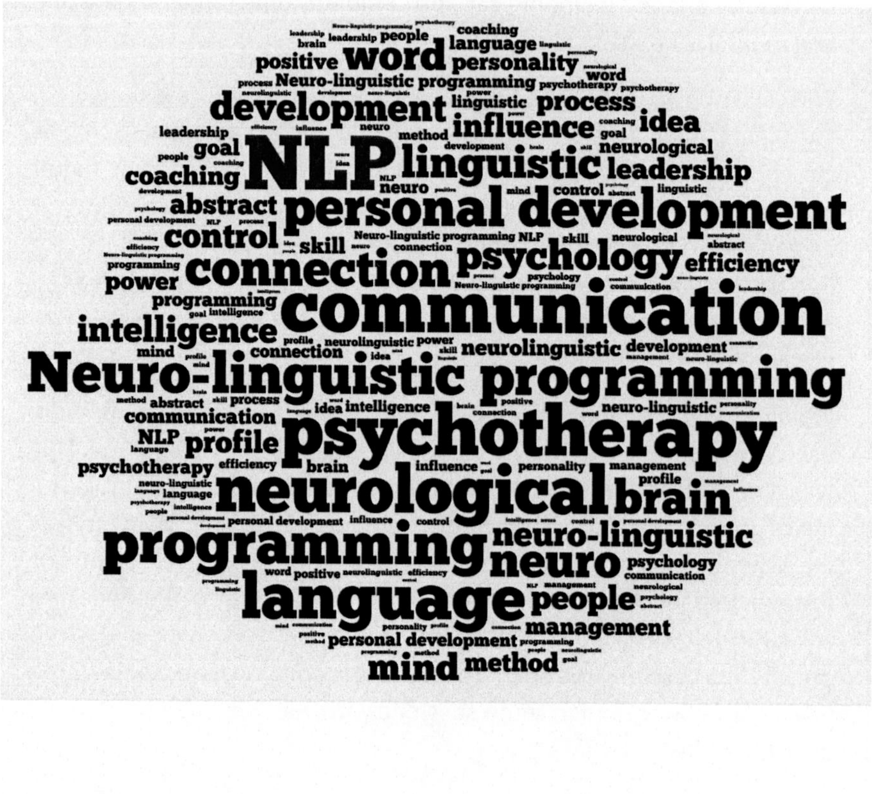
coaching
leadership
people
language
brain
positive
word
personality
word
Neuro-linguistic programming
psychotherapy
development
linguistic
process
influence
idea
leadership
method
goal
neurological
NLP
linguistic
leadership
coaching
neuro
control
abstract
personal development
control
skill
Neuro-linguistic programming NLP
psychology
efficiency
connection
power
programming
communication
intelligence
neurolinguistic
development
mind
Neuro-linguistic programming
abstract
process
idea
intelligence
neuro-linguistic
communication
psychotherapy
NLP
profile
psychotherapy
efficiency
brain
influence
personality
management
profile
neuro-linguistic
language
neurological
brain
personal development
programming
neuro-linguistic
neuro
psychology
communication
language
people
management
personal development
mind
method

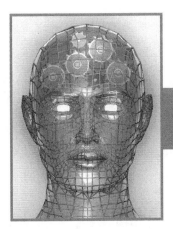

CHAPTER 3

What Can You Do with NLP?

P erhaps a better question is what can you not do with NLP? The short answer is, not much. NLP is universally applicable because it is concerned with individual subjective experience. Although feelings and experiences vary widely from person to person, both are experienced by every person.

NLP can be used for any task concerned with self-improvement or individual change. This includes improving confidence, reducing anxiety, delivering a presentation, eliminating unwanted behaviors, and enjoying deeper relationships with your friends and family. The positive effects of NLP, which you may begin to apply in one area of you life, say, academics, will ripple into others, and raise the entire quality of your life. In the same way that when one part of your life is going wrong, it effects other parts, NLP can spread the positivity around your whole life like butter on bread.

To be clear, NLP should never be a replacement for therapy. You should never say to yourself: "I think I need therapy, but I'll do NLP instead!" No. NLP should rather be a supplement to any necessary therapeutic treatments. That said, NLP is great because of its immediate application. You can start on the bus, in your room, at the cafeteria, or even your local coffee shop. That's because NLP hones in on specific targets, rather than diagnosing why and moving past serious issues that are for more clinical settings. The question with NLP is: "How can I create change in my life? What thoughts, behaviors, and practices can I rehearse over and over until they bring me success?"

During NLP sessions, clients have the opportunity to identify problems or concerns as they see them. Conversations between the client and practitioner or therapist focus on what is happening now and what the client would like to happen in the future. The client is then invited to step into the feelings and experiences of accomplishing his or her desired goal. You can (and are encouraged to) do this at home; use your journal as you process what is happening and plan what you would like to happen. Each section in this chapter is devoted to a specific area that you may or may not chose to target with the methods of NLP, methods which have been covered briefly and will be discussed in more detail in the following chapters.

So, back to the question of what you can do with NLP. This chapter will provide a general overview of the areas of your life that can be improved with a dedication to NLP experiences.

What Do You Want NLP to Do for You?

Remember reading the presupposition "Everyone has the resources they need to make the changes they want" from Chapter 1? When you are ready to begin creating changes in your life, it is enough to start by embracing that realization. It does not matter if you have not yet identified or connected with the resources that will get you those changes. Just know they are there.

You know you want to make a change. Maybe you have a problem with self-image and can't see the beauty that's there in mirror every morning. Maybe you get bogged down with foggy thinking, shame, or doubt when you do your homework every night (hence the constant getting up for "phone breaks" every five minutes). Maybe you can't seem to make any friends that you actually like due to your own inner turmoil, which in turn, attracts people with similar problems. There's a problem, yes? You think about it all the time, right? Well, for every problem there *is* a solution.

Take your journal out (that we both know you have right in front of you, right?) and decide on two or three problems in your life that are taking up all your energy. What are you dwelling on? What's holding you back? You can pick more later, but pick two or three for your first time reading the book and another handful on the second reading. Whatever you've listed, chances are it will be addressed in this chapter, and if not, you'll gain the tools to address them with NLP technique. If you're having trouble deciding (maybe NLP can help you with your indecisiveness!), read the chapter all the way through and participate in the exercises (remember, this isn't a traditional "book:" it's meant to be interactive.

To kick-off, start with this exercise. Remember, these exercises take courage and honesty in order to get anything from them.

Exercise 1: Changing Your Map of an Experience

The following is a technique you can use to change bothersome feelings. This strategy for problem solving employs some of the techniques used with behavioral therapy. This is a very easy exercise to try at home.

Step 1: Recreate an experience where you felt ashamed, humiliated, or angry. Imagine yourself having that experience right now. Step into every detail of that event, engaging your senses as you feel the experience. Name the primary feeling that comes to you as accurately as you can. Now, rate the feeling a number on a scale from one to 10, with 10 being the most intense.

Step 2: Choose a song that expresses a feeling completely unlike the feeling you experienced during the event. Let's say you picked the feeling of "hopelessness." A good song would then be "Happy" by Pharell Williams.

Step 3: Now, step back into that same experience. Only this time, hear song you choose playing in the background. Again, make the experience as vivid as you can. Let the music play loud and clear. You may even have to struggle to hear people talking over the music, or you may be so distracted by the bouncy tune that you give more attention to the song than to what is happening.

Step 4: Vividly imagine yourself having the experience once more. This time, imagine the scene without the music. Notice any changes in your feelings. Many people notice that the unpleasant feeling has shifted. It may not feel as serious or hurtful. You may even feel that you can laugh about the event now. Check your rating again on a scale from one to 10, with 10 being the most intense. Has the number moved at all? If you notice no changes, do not worry. Continue the exercise using different songs — do not be afraid to try wacky or animal sounds as well — until you find one that helps you release the unpleasant feeling.

Pretty easy, right? The key here is to give yourself over to or step into the experience as if it is happening in the moment. Have you ever heard the expression, "If I had it to do over..."? This exercise provides an opportunity to have the experience again to change the outcome — or at least your internal coding of it. Changing your internal coding of the experience changes the way you think and feel about what happened. Make sure to write down the reflections you gather from each step in the process so that they remain accessible to you later on.

Now let's move on to the areas of your life where you may be able to apply this NLP exercise, and many more, to achieve your goals!

Using NLP to Improve the Educational Experience

Whether you want to own up to it or not, everyone's experience as a student is made ten times better if your teacher likes you. You don't even have to be particularly excellent in a subject for a teacher to like you! You could just be a good person with good habits, awareness, and decisive thinking that makes you a pleasure to be around. So what are some ways you can heighten your experience at school? Start with these four strategies.

- **Use behavioral flexibility.** Don't stay stuck in your ways in class, especially if you're the kid sulking in your seat all the time. Put the way you act under the spotlight for a second and try changing what you think needs to be changed. Maybe the teacher has told you several times to straighten up, and you ignored them. Now is the time to straighten up. Act like your head is being pulled up by a thread. Once you make this little change, move onto the next one. Maybe it's raising your hand once a week. Perfect! And if you're unsure of the ways you could improve your behavior, ask the teacher: "What are some habits you think I need to develop in order to succeed?" Take their answers, and keep asking yourself questions and adjusting your behavior.

- **Practice sensory awareness**. Do you notice what is going on within and around you? Can you use this information to manage communication? This is particularly important in the classroom. Your teachers and fellow peers pick up on messages you send out, whether you know you're sending them or not. They make decisions based on your body language, facial cues, and tone of voice. So be mindful of how you are coming across. You can check this by watching how they respond. If they seem to scoff at you or avert their gaze, adjust yourself into a more comfortable and confident posture. Make sure the way you're holding yourself is the way you want to be perceived!

- **Build rapport**. Have you taken a moment to determine if you are thinking useful thoughts? Do you know what your current state is and how it will impact the other pillars? Recall that the four pillars are rapport, outcome thinking, sensory awareness, and behavioral flexibility. Remember that when you are not in a resourceful state, you can trigger an anchor to quickly return to one. Before beginning your day and during each break, decide which state would be the most useful for the next part of your day. Name the state. Do you need to be calm and comforting or silly and light? Use a predetermined anchor to get into your state and watch the quality of your experience at school improve dramatically.

Promote Positive Learning Behaviors

NLP is an excellent tool for determining what type of learner you are. This alone can be very helpful because it creates a win-win situation: students experience more effective learning and teachers more effectively teach students.

The way you discover what kind of learner you are is by engaging in the techniques in this book and using just a little bit of self-reflection. As you engage with your memories, you'll learn about *how* you remember. Do you remember more of what people *say* and tend to *hear* your memories than see them? Do you tend towards remembering strong visualizations or physical sensations? The way you remember will define your learning style and how you'll get the most out of school. It *does* make up about half of your waking life at this point, doesn't it?

The following is a brief introduction each learning style and how you can make the most of each, no matter which category you fall under.

Visual learners

These students retain more of what they see than what they hear and do not usually find noise to be a distraction. For example, these learners typically respond well to maps, graphs, charts, and tables. When trying to sit down for a long study session, try to pull the material in by asking yourself to "visualize" the information and frame your answers to questions beginning with "I see."

Auditory learners

Auditory learners often find noise to be a distraction as they retain more of what they hear rather than what they see. They are also generally better at oral than written tasks. If you're an auditory learner, you are most likely the one chatting it up on the sly in the classroom. For your own benefit, make sure to incorporate auditory methods into your academic work. This might mean reading aloud, talking about what you've learned to yourself, and making things rhyme in order to remember them.

Kinesthetic learners

Kinesthetic learners prefer hands-on learning experiences. They find it difficult to sit still for long periods and want to show more than tell. Kinesthetic learners experience feelings and sensations in response to stimulus. These students love to get their hands on things and appreciate opportunities for movement. When studying, make sure to incorporate "movement breaks" for your study sessions. You'll do better if you allow yourself to move around and change up the scenery during your study sessions (that goes for everyone!).

Exercise 2: Recoding Bad Experiences

OK onto the second exercise! You're ready with that journal and pen, right?

Take a moment and use the following exercise to recode a bad experience. Recoding allows you to identify your current feelings about an experience and change the way you describe and feel about that experience. Going off of the topic of learning and learning styles, maybe think of a memory from a class that played your weaknesses. Maybe you're a visual learner and were required to write a ten page paper that you flunked and want to process the feelings of failure. It doesn't really matter, just as long as it involves a memory and a negative emotion.

Step 1: Create two columns on a piece of paper. Label one column "How I feel about what happened" and the other column "How I would like to feel about what happened." You will not need to write about what happened, only how you would like to feel about the experience.

Step 2: Write at least three to five feeling words in each column. The following are some examples of feeling words that you might use:

How I feel about what happened:

- Angry
- Frustrated
- Not supported

How I would like to feel about what happened:

- Understanding
- Resourceful
- Supported

Step 3: Breathe deeply. Ask yourself if your current feelings are useful. Ask yourself if you need to change your feelings, and what the benefit of changing your feelings would be. Are you dwelling? Would you feel liberated if you moved on to become more resourceful, understanding, etc.?

Step 4: Focus on how you feel about what happened. See the feelings as light. As you breathe deeply, see the lights begin to dim. Notice any tension in your body as you move through this step.

Step 5: Now think about how you would like to feel about what happened. Experience the feelings as radiant energy you take in with each breath; the more deeply you breath, the more you take in the good feelings. Continue this process until you feel the way you would like to feel.

Step 6: Return to your written list. Cross out everything in column one and read column two aloud. For example, say to yourself, "I feel resourceful." You might further reinforce this feeling by providing evidence to yourself. .

With time, this exercise will become part of an automatic strategy repertoire for managing feelings around bad experiences. NLP gives you the tools to be deliberate about how you choose to respond to everything that happens within and around you. Again, this isn't just strictly "school-related." Surely, there is ample room for life to disappoint you. Life is real, and we mean *really* real, so please feel free to use experiences from your family life, interactions with peers and friends, and seriously almost anything else. Chances are, you'll find lots of memories that you're still grappling with to this day, no matter if they happened five or ten years ago. Each would benefit from the implementation of this exercise.

However, coming back to the original topic of this section, the way you learn and remember information, and how and what you remember will define your experience in both school and life. We provided a very brief definition of "framing" in Chapter 1: the attitude and beliefs you derive from a certain experience. If you have a generally very negative and dismissive attitude, then chances are you won't really learn anything: how to deal with people, how to memorize facts to do well on a taste, and so on. So if you find yourself struggling in school or at home for whatever reason — maybe you can't remember things because you're classes aren't taught according to your learning style or maybe your parents have to tell you the same thing over and over again, it's always important to try and "reframe." Take a look:

Reframing

At any given time, we are faced with so much information that it is impossible to consciously take it all in. Imagine that the events that happen in your life as vast as the sky. The information you consciously take in is said to be within your "frame." You put a frame around the portion of sky or information that you consciously take in. Reframing allows you to consider more and/or different information. Imagining the sky again, reframing is much like enlarging, or shifting, the original frame. Reframing provides a different perspective from which more possibilities or choices emerge.

Using NLP in Your Personal Life

When ready to embark on any change or accomplish any goal, it is important to understand at least three things:

- How the goal fits into the journey of your life. Is this goal you're choosing on the way to where you want to end up in five or ten years from now?

- What beliefs hold you back from taking this journey?

- Which beliefs do you need to give you the fuel to reach this next step in your life?

Consider each of these questions as you move through the next section on NLP in personal life.

Dissociation to eliminate fear

One of the things holding you back from your desired destination in life could very well be fear.

Releasing fears or painful memories is not simply a matter of showing your thoughts who is boss; it is about changing the feelings associated with the thoughts. NLP is effective for releasing painful memories or overcoming fears using *association and dissociation.* Association is experiencing or seeing the world through your own body. Dissociation is experiencing or seeing the world from outside of your own body or as an observer. NLP tools take the pain away from difficult memories by helping individuals learn to dissociate painful feelings from the bad experience and associate the experience with neutral or even positive feelings.

Take out your journal again! To dissociate from phobias or painful memories, see yourself experiencing the difficult memory on a screen or in a picture. See the picture as an interested observer — dissociated from it — rather than as the person having the experience — associated with it. Imagine the picture or screen moving farther away, becoming blurry and less clear. As the picture fades, verbally release the feeling. For example, think to yourself, "I release any feelings of anger." As you release the unwanted feelings, verbally invite wanted feelings by telling yourself, "I choose to feel peaceful." Try the exercise with several different unwanted feelings. You will find that when you separate the feeling from the experience you eliminate painful feelings.

Now, what about irrational fears that you have that don't have any rational basis? If you suffer from any kind of phobia or what any practitioner would refer to as an "irrational fear" (let's say, a fear of apple pies, a fear that doesn't make any sense because apple pies are quite frankly delicious), dissociation would be useful as well. Simple imagine the object of this fear as a picture or movie, and repeat the steps laid out above.

Decrease stress and anxiety

Relieving stress and anxiety is about more than thinking calm and peaceful thoughts. "Mapping across," an important tool developed by NLP founders Bandler and Grinder, is useful for decreasing anxiety and stress. Mapping across allows you to transfer an identity or skill from one situation to another.

For example, suppose Susan is great with customers at work, even difficult ones. She does a good job communicating, she is able to pace herself when customers shout angrily, and she can lead them into calmer states. Yet at home, Susan cannot seem to have a civil conversation with her teenage daughter (sound familiar?). Mapping across allows Susan to identify the strong people skills she has in one setting and enlist them to improve communication in the setting where she is having trouble.

The goal here is for Susan to bring her identity as a competent communicator into interactions with her daughter. Susan can do this by triggering the state she uses at work in interactions with her daughter, so she establishes an anchor that is associated with the state she is in at work. She decides her anchor is putting her hand on her shoulder when there's an angry customer and she calms them down. After a while, she then places her hand on her shoulder when she's trying to communicate calmly with her daughter.

So now that you're familiar with mapping, think about your familiarity with stress and anxiety, which tend to peak or keep increasing in young adulthood and adulthood. Think about a time when you felt rejected by a group of people (one of the strongest negative feelings we possess is shame). Or when you had an incredibly intense fight with one of your parents. Maybe you have a fear of failure which is causing you anxiety every time you're given an exam or assignment. Then think about when you're able to relax and create an anchor. Practice this and hopefully you'll make more room for happiness and less for stress.

Eliminate unwanted behaviors

It takes more than willpower to eliminate unwanted behaviors like overeating or procrastinating. We all want to make important changes in our lives that help us feel better, achieve more success, and enjoy deeper connections with the people we care about. That we often fail in making these changes is not a matter of wanting something impossible or unattainable; it is a matter of approach.

When it comes to making life changes, our efforts must focus on strategies such as aligning, associating, and visualizing rather than wishing, agonizing, and struggling. Creating change of any type is absolutely possible when you begin from within. Think about something that you have tried to change in the past. Perhaps you wanted to quit overeating. Remember the moment you made the decision. Maybe even write it down or say it aloud. Think about how you felt and what you were thinking as you made the decision. If you were not able to eliminate the habit, chances are that in addition to the excitement or hopefulness you felt about being addiction free, you also felt fear, doubt, or anxiety.

Doing something different requires congruence. With congruence, all of your thoughts, goals, and behaviors are in agreement. We will review the example of overeating to demonstrate. The goal was to stop overeating, but the behavior, which may have included cravings and feelings of hunger, did not support the goal. Also, your thoughts, which may have sounded like, "This is harder than I thought," "I do not know how else to handle my stress," and "It is not fair to my friends or family that I am so irritable," did not support the goal. Given that the thoughts, behavior, and goal about overeating were at odds or incongruent, it is unlikely that the goal will be accomplished.

That's why before embarking on an arduous journey to your goal, you have to sit in the military tents a bit and strategize your approach. What's a mantra you can say to combat your negative thoughts? Maybe: "I am my most prized possession. I can't afford to lose it." What will be your response to uncomfortable thoughts and how will you replace the comfort that the unhealthy habit once provided you?

Reprocessing

Reprocessing helps us become less reactive by turning a badly coded experience into one with good coding. Some memories, particularly difficult or vivid ones, are "badly coded." Bad code also becomes part of our belief system. Long held beliefs, whether based on good code or bad code, are rarely challenged; they feel like second nature or a part of who we are and the reason for what we do. Reprocessing is a powerful tool for behavior modification.

You may have noticed that as you try and recode, reframe, and develop more positive behaviors, you're faced battling an "inner critic." When you do the exercises, you hear a very loud and arrogant: "This is stupid!" And it is difficult, especially if your inner critic is bossy and loud, to focus on anything other than that voice. The following exercise helps you quiet the critic so you can hear thoughts that support you in taking action for change and get the most out of reprocessing and the other activities in this book.

CASE STUDY: A reprocessing example

According to the National Public Radio news show *All Things Considered*, fear of clowns, or coulrophobia, is among the top three phobias in Britain. Surprisingly, the other two phobias involve spiders and needles — not flying.

A June 17, 2010 interview on the show with Paul Carpenter of John Lawson's Circus in the U.K., who performs as Popol the clown, tells of his work to help people eliminate their fear of clowns. The sessions, called clownseling, help those with the phobia reprocess by changing what they think and believe about clowns. Participants come into the circus before the crowds and noise and before the clowns get into costume. They have the opportunity to watch the transformation as performers put on their makeup and costumes. If all goes well, participants can even don their own clown costume and makeup. These clownseling sessions help those with coulrophobia tell themselves a new story about clowns, thus giving them the ability to recode their beliefs and change their behavior on encountering clowns.

Exercise 3: How to Address Your Inner Critic

The following six steps can help you gain the support of the inner voice that says, "I can't," so that you can devote all your resources to discovering how you can. Have your journal on hand for this one; you will need it.

Step 1: Hear the inner voice in clear detail including the tone, pitch, and words. Is it a voice you recognize? Maybe the voice is repeating negative thoughts or criticisms someone in your life has leveled against you.

Step 2: Ask the critical voice to share the positive intention it is trying to achieve with its criticism. You may need to continue questioning until you find agreement with the positive intention. Maybe the positive intention is to protect you from failure. Remind yourself and the voice: There is no failure, only feedback. Ask until the positive intention is clear.

Step 3: Thank the critical voice for sharing the positive intention. Yes, you read that right: *Thank the critical voice.* You want to begin to notice and manage your feelings, where before you may have fought with and rejected them.

Step 4: Ask if your inner critic is open to exploring any other possibilities for achieving the positive intention. The answer may not be immediately clear. Being willing to consider the question will help you to stop feeling stuck.

Step 5: Enlist the support of the voice in discovering other possibilities. Choose several of the best possibilities that calm the voice. You do not have to make a decision at this point. You are simply considering your options, and when you remember that the map is not the territory, you know that your options — like you — are unlimited.

Step 6: See yourself vividly experiencing each of the best outcomes. Base your final choice on the outcomes that feel most "right" or comfortable. You should not have a nagging feeling. If you feel any doubt or resistance in any part of your body, pay attention. This likely means you do not have cooperation from your subconscious mind. If the subconscious mind says "no," the plan will not go forward successfully.

Increase Productivity with NLP

NLP can increase productivity because it supports clear communication. When you are clear about what you want and how best to communicate that to the listener, the opportunities for miscommunication and wasted efforts are reduced. How are productivity and communication related?

- Communication makes it easy to spot knowledge gaps. The bottom line is that people perform better when they have a full understanding of the work with which they are tasked; better performance equals higher productivity. For example, does the team member understand how his or her task fits into the larger picture? Can the team member describe his or her responsibilities?

- Communication also helps you understand how people learn. NLP helps you speak the unique language of the person you are talking to, which improves learning. People with confidence in their ability to learn a task are more likely to pick up the task and even adapt their skills for better efficiency. For example, when teaching someone to complete a new task or giving directions, it is helpful to know whether they will respond better if you show him or her rather than tell him or her what to do.

- Communication helps build teams that are more resourceful and supportive, thus creating win-win scenarios. In a win-win scenario, everyone feels at least something they value or think of as important has been addressed. When people feel heard, acknowledged, and included, they are more motivated to perform at their best level. The opposite of this principle was illustrated in June 2010 when Miramar, Florida-based Spirit Airlines cancelled several flights, stranding passengers. Why? Because communications between the airline and the pilot's union failed to result in a win-win solution on pay.

The Value of NLP in Improving Relationships

NLP provides the tools for building strong communication skills that improve relationships and personal success. One of the best ways to improve communications skills and personal relationships is to learn how to build rapport. Rapport is simply creating alignment or connection with another person. When there is no rapport, there is often resistance, misunderstanding, and feelings of not being heard or understood. When you build rapport, you foster feelings of understanding, familiarity, and appreciation — feelings to which most people respond positively.

You can build rapport by using matching and mirroring, which involves adopting the same posture or tone of voice as the person with whom you are interacting. You can achieve rapport by letting your behavior reflect the state you want others to feel about you. For example, do you want others to experience you as compassionate, confident, concerned or angry, anxious, and self-centered? Find ways to present yourself the way you want to be perceived.

How to Design a Well-formed Goal

Start by being very clear about what you want. Use positive language to state what you want. For example, instead of saying, "I do not want to be a loner anymore," say, "I want to be more social." Phrasing is important here because it shifts the focus from what you do not want to what you do want. NLP has come up with six things to consider when designing a goal with the best chance for success. Use the following list when developing your own goals:

1. **Determine if what you want is fully within your control.** If any portion of your goal requires change or action from someone other than you, you cannot be fully in control of the outcome. Your goal should also be possible for you. For example, though it may be possible to improve your ability to play basketball, it may not be possible to compete with Michael Jordan.

2. **Decide how you will know when your goal has been accomplished.** You are more likely to have evidence of success if your goals are measureable.

3. **Review the larger impact of your goal to determine if the goal fits into your life as it is at this time.** In other words, look at the whole of your life and the important people in it. How and what will be affected as you work toward your goal? What fallout or obstacles do you anticipate? Planning ahead can help you successfully navigate those obstacles, thus improving your chances for success.

4. **Create a compelling future. See yourself moving along the path toward your goal.** Imagine where you are right now and see yourself moving until you get to where you want to go. Once you are there, give yourself over to the experience of the achievement. Allow yourself to revel in the sights, sounds, tastes, smells, words, colors, and weather. Use all of your senses to fully enter into the experience of the achievement.

5. **Develop your plan.** Now that you have your plan in place, it is time to fast-forward to the feeling of accomplishment. Pretending that the goal has already been accomplished makes it feel more real. Use the following steps to anticipate the success feelings that will come with meeting your goal:

   - **Visit your goal.** Vividly experience the joy and pride of achieving your goal.

   - **See your future.** Notice how achieving your goal has improved your life.

   - **See your past.** Retrace the path you took to get to your future. Notice how the journey has changed you.

   - **Walk back along your path.** Recall what you did to achieve your goal. Remember the support you had and how you encouraged yourself.

   - **Notice the steps along your path.** Recall the resources and abilities you marshaled to achieve your goal, the order of steps you used, and the time it took.

- **Focus on now.** You should have a full appreciation of what it will take to reach your goal and how it will feel to achieve your goal.

6. **Run through a dress rehearsal.** Most significant accomplishments happen at least twice: once in the mind and again in reality. The first time the goal is accomplished is a dress rehearsal of sorts. The dress rehearsal provides confidence that success is possible. The dress rehearsal also provides another opportunity to experience the feelings of success associated with meeting a goal. Use the following steps to imagine you have already met your goal:

  - **Assume the role.** Use the language, thoughts, and postures that are associated with your new role.

  - **Walk the path.** Trace the path that led you to your goal. See yourself at the end of the path looking back to the beginning.

  - **"Beam" yourself back.** Retrace your steps on the path so that you are back at the beginning. See the steps in front of you as doable.

Taking Action

Accomplishing a goal requires planning for accountability. Being accountable helps you set important time limits and establish a list of tasks that you can check off as you make progress toward your goal. The following are the steps to take in creating your plan for accountability:

- **Make a date.** I will begin working on my goal on January 1. I will complete my goal by June 1.

- **Establish benchmarks.** Break your goal into steps that can be accomplished in the short term. For example, "I will find an exercise partner by June 15 or week one," and "I will have lost four pounds by month one or July 15." Set a reminder on your phone or write and post your dates where you can see them.

- **Stay focused on your vision.** See yourself at various stages along the path to goal completion, visualize yourself completing your goal, and imagine what you will look like and how you will feel after your goal has been accomplished. Remember to engage all of your senses in the experience so it feels as if you have achieved the goal before it is accomplished.

- **Get started.** Even the best plan is meaningless unless it is paired with action. You must start your plan and work through it step-by-step to complete it successfully.

The following exercise will help you take action when you find your motivation waning or just plain missing.

Exercise 4: Motivating Yourself to Take Action

Sometimes it seems the to-do list grows in direct proportion to waning motivation to tackle it. Manage yourself in the classroom as well as in your administrative responsibilities. Try the following exercise to motivate yourself to tackle tasks with enthusiasm instead of half-hearted dread:

The Godiva® Chocolate pattern is named for the intense feelings of desire and pleasure lush chocolate inspires. This technique helps the user transfer or associate positive feelings from an activity that is enjoyed to an activity that is not enjoyed to create motivation for doing it.

Use the Godiva Chocolate pattern to motivate yourself when faced with a task you are dreading.

Step 1: Think of something you are very excited about. It could be something you have done or something you fantasize about doing. See, hear, and feel yourself having this wonderful experience. The image in your mind is called Picture 1.

Step 2: Take a break and observe your surroundings. The goal here is to break state. Breaking state is simply moving out of the feelings or state of mind that you are experiencing in the moment.

Step 3: Think of the task you are dreading. See yourself completing the task or imagine as if you are observing yourself doing the task. This is Picture 2.

Step 4: Check in with yourself to see if Picture 2 is what you really want. It is important to stop and notice how you are feeling at this point. Are there any feelings of objection in your mind or body? In other words, is there any reason you do not want to enjoy the task for which you are trying to create motivation? If so, you will need to work through or reframe your objections before you can move forward. See the sidebar to read about reframing.

Step 5: Place Picture 2, the activity you are not enthusiastic about yet, behind Picture 1 in your mind. Do this by imagining two photographs on a clothing rack. Picture 2 should be positioned behind Picture 1 on the rack.

Step 6: Imagine a connection between the pictures sitting on the clothing rack in your mind. While doing this, create a small hole in Picture 1. It should be just large enough that you can see Picture 2 through the hole.

Step 7: Allow all the images and feelings from Picture 1 to spill through the hole onto Picture 2. Picture 1 will begin to cover Picture 2, and you will begin to transfer the excitement you feel from Picture 1 to Picture 2.

Step 8: Keeping the excitement in place, imagine yourself closing the hole.

Step 9: Repeat as needed until the feelings associated with Picture 1 become completely associated with Picture 2.

Perceptual Positions

Perceptual positions are like viewpoints or places from which we interpret information. Different positions provide different views or perspectives about what is happening and how it is understood. Perceptual positions help us with visualization and are critical for association and dissociation. There are five positions:

- **First position:** This is the associated position. From here, you fully experience what is happening in your own body and through your own eyes. You allow yourself to feel, see, and hear what is going on and use that information to stand grounded in your inner power.

- **Second position:** This position gives you the perspective of the person you are communicating with. From here, you try to imagine how you sound, look, and feel to the person you are interacting with. You are stepping into that person's shoes to gain insight into how he or she is experiencing you.

- **Third position:** This is the dissociated position. This position allows you to be objective or detached from emotions, particularly difficult ones. Assuming this position is almost like watching a movie, you observe rather than participate.

- **Fourth position:** This position provides an overview perspective. From here, you are concerned with understanding what is going on with all of the participants and the system that connects them.

- **Fifth position:** This is the cosmic view or transcendent view. This position is most easily achieved through meditation.

You can use perceptual positions to improve confidence, reduce anxiety, or create your desired state.

Work to align your perceptual positions. For example, when in first position, you should not project your thoughts or feelings onto the second position. This is often how miscommunication occurs; we decide how another person feels or what he or she is thinking instead of letting that person communicate his or her own feelings. What you should hear from second position is what that person is thinking and feeling and not what you think or feel.

No, NLP does not give you the power to read minds.

It does help you become attuned to clues about what a person might be thinking or feeling based on body language and word choice. If you are uncertain about how to interpret what you see or hear, do not be afraid to clarify with the speaker.

The following is a basic example. Suppose you are talking with someone who briskly runs his or her hands along their arms. If you are not sure whether he or she has a sudden case of "goose bumps" or is simply chilly, you can ask. Likewise, if you are giving an afternoon talk and a participant yawns, it would be inappropriate to immediately conclude he or she is yawning because your presentation is boring. He or she might have yawned because your workshop falls just after the conference luncheon or even because of medication. Aligning perceptual positions allows us to look for clues rather than arrive at false conclusions.

Improve self-image

Poor self-image requires changing your internal representation, or the way you think of yourself. Your thoughts create your reality. To move past your own mental limitations, you must change your mind.

Many of the presuppositions of NLP are designed to help individuals use strength-based explanations when examining their behaviors. These positive ways of talking about yourself remind you that even if you have made mistakes, you are still capable of achieving success. For example, if you subscribe to the ideas that people are not broken, they work perfectly, and every behavior has a positive intent:

- You can acknowledge your innate perfection.

- You can immediately stop beating yourself up.

- You can instead start looking for useful behavior to replace the dysfunctional behavior you previously used to get at your intent.

If you know that you are more than your behavior:

- You know that who you are (lovable, complete, and worthy, for example) is not at all related to what you do. And...

If you know that there is no failure, only feedback:

- You can look for the lessons hidden in what you previously called failures.

- You can use that feedback to find new strategies to get you what you want.

- You can begin to see yourself as someone in process of accomplishing a goal or building a skill, rather than as a failure.

Much like you can visualize yourself meeting other goals such as improving your performance, you can visualize yourself feeling like you want to feel about yourself. Step into the experience of accomplishing your goal as if it is happening.

Another strategy for building self-esteem is to imagine how someone that really loves you or has deep appreciation for you feels about you. Add those feelings and thoughts to your beliefs about yourself.

The Circle of Excellence Pattern

One way to develop more esteem and appreciation for yourself is to practice the Circle of Excellence pattern. This pattern helps you harness inner resources, such as confidence, so that they can be applied whenever the need arises. You can use the Circle of Excellence pattern to move out of negative states. Remember that a state describes how you are in body and mind at a given moment. Examples of states you may be in include confident, joyful, angry, or calm.

Exercise 5: Using the Circle of Excellence to Access Inner Resources

Use this exercise to get from where you are — perhaps a negative state such as angry, to a positive state, such as centered and calm — using the Circle of Excellence pattern.

Step 1: First, look for triggers. What are the visual, auditory, or kinesthetic cues that led to the negative state? Maybe you always become upset when you hear a certain word, phrase, or sound that your friends, sibling, parent, fellow student, or teacher makes.

Step 2: Next, draw an imaginary circle on the floor. Think of a time when you felt centered and calm. Allow the memory to help you experience the same feelings right now.

Step 3: As you continue experiencing the positive feelings, step into the circle. As you move into the circle, begin to recall the anchors that precede the negative state. The key is to hold onto the positive feelings while simultaneously recalling the negative triggers. If you have sufficiently amplified your positive state, it will feel more powerful than the negative triggers. The negative triggers will thus be extinguished.

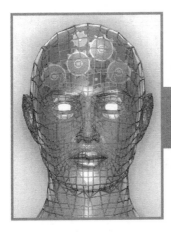

CHAPTER 4

The Pillars of NLP

Rapport, sensory acuity, behavioral flexibility, and outcome thinking form the four pillars of NLP. These pillars are the basis for the NLP philosophy. Think of them as four essential skills that you should be continually developing as you practice NLP exercises and learn about NLP philosophy.

Behavioral Flexibility

As the word flexibility suggests, this pillar is concerned with one's ability to adapt his or her actions as a strategy for influencing a particular response from and in response to another person. Behavioral flexibility allows you to feel comfortable with diverse groups of people and in a variety of circumstances because your behavior is motivated by a desire to influence, understand, connect, and build rapport. Behavioral flexibility is much like redirecting your course; it allows you to change course or choose different ways of relating to others if your actions are not leading you in the intended direction. For example, being flexible with behavior can be as simple as moving to stand closer to someone that seems upset. It can also look like adjusting a training format to increase interaction if participants do not seem responsive. The key with behavioral flexibility is noticing the level of responsiveness, deciding if it is high enough, and if not, adapting behavior to improve results.

Sensory Acuity

Can you tell what a person is thinking and feeling before they even say a word? You can see it in his or her eyes or maybe the way the person holds the shoulders or positions the arms. You can use your senses to assess the efficacy of communication. Paying attention to small changes in facial expression or eye movement helps us determine if what we are saying resonates with or annoys others. It is important to note here that body language is as unique as individuals themselves. Though it is true that some signals, such as crossed arms, may mean the same thing for many people, most meaning should be discovered and interpreted through active observation.

This rule is particularly important when interacting with people who may not share your cultural background. Do not make assumptions about what you see. Continue to check what you see against what you hear and feel. This is called calibration, a sort of fine-tuning process that helps you get in sync during communication. Think of this process similarly to how you might think of each instrument in an orchestra tuning to one pitch. Tuning allows the instruments to play together in harmony. In interactions, calibration or tuning allows each person to follow the pitch or cue for better communication.

CASE STUDY:
The Power of Beliefs

Emily Sands, a student who has studied at Princeton and Harvard, conducted a year-long study on gender bias within the theater community. In one of these studies, Sands provided literary managers and artistic directors throughout the country with the same scripts. The only difference in these scripts was the name of the author: one half was given a male name and the other a female name. Although the scripts were exactly identical, those scripts that appeared to be written by a female author were rated consistently lower.

What does this study suggest about the power of beliefs and how they not only shape us, but shape our sensory acuity? Our beliefs function much like the lines on the road or highway. We stay within the boundaries of the lines, even when the boundaries confine us or limit us, because we do not see anything else. Imagine the kinds of movies, plays, stories, music, and all the like that we're missing out on simply due to closing our senses off.

Rapport

You may recall the presupposition: "The meaning of your communication is the response you get." When there is misunderstanding or resistance, the likely reason is lack of rapport. The goal in creating rapport is not wholesale agreement of everything that is being communicated, but rather to show the other person that you understand what they are trying to communicate.

You have no doubt shared a conversation that just flowed or met someone and felt that you had known each other for years. If so, then you understand rapport. It is the difference between a conversation that feels awkward or uncomfortable and one that does not. When you notice that the conversation is uncomfortable, use the pillars of NLP, as well as the individual's output channels, to begin building rapport.

The output channels are words, voice, and body. To get a full understanding of what is being communicated, you must survey, interpret, and respond to all three output channels.

1. The words:

- Does the person use expressions that feel familiar to you?
- Which sensory words does the person use?

2. The voice:

- How loud or soft is the person's voice?
- What can you tell from the tone of voice?
- Is he or she speaking fast or slow?

3. The body:

- How are the arms and legs positioned?
- What gestures are being used?
- How has the speaker positioned his or her body in relation to yours?
- What can you learn from his or her facial expressions?

UCLA Professor Emeritus of Psychology Albert Mehrabian assigned weights or values to each of the three output channels. Born in 1939, Mehrabian's studies of communication led to what is today known as the 7-38-55 rule. In short, words account for seven percent of communication, while voice and body account for 38 percent and 55 percent, respectively.

The message is not that words do not matter; they do. Instead, the message is that words must be congruent with tone of voice and body language to build rapport. You will recall that congruence in communication is another way of saying that your words match your behavior and tone of voice. When they don't, the listener will ultimately take his or her cues about what you are really thinking and feeling from your voice and body, not your words. For example, if you offer a friend a compliment in a sarcastic tone, they will most likely discount the words and take meaning from your tone of voice.

You should respond to outputs by matching or mirroring what you see and hear. In doing this you are not behaving like a copycat; rather, you are sending a signal or demonstrating a pattern that the listener will recognize as familiar. The practice of matching another person's predicates, or words that reveal how he or she represents things in his or her consciousness, behavior, speech, and posture is called pacing.

Outcome Thinking

For every shadow in the world, there is a light responsible for it, no matter how confusing it may be to find it in the chaos that is life. Remember that the darkness is a distraction that negativity will naturally pull your attention, but it's up to you to whip your head around and charge on. Dwelling on problems is simply not useful; charging towards the outcome is.

Once you decide what's important in life, then it can be applied to almost anything. If you're a young adult, you're probably a student, living with your parents, playing around with different hobbies, finding out what you do or don't like. Let's say you're trying to master a musical instrument and eventually you want to perform at an open mic night. You might have a number of problems with this: you're nervous, you're not hitting the right notes, and you get frustrated easily.

Learning new things puts us all in a vulnerable but humbling spot. We're openly admitting we don't know something, that we're deficient in some fashion, and emotions are likely to come up, especially if you're a particularly emotional person. You're in the dark: you don't know if you can do it, if you'll blow the audience away at your local coffee shop, and you keep feeling inadequate, frustrated, and ashamed. What is it that will pull you through?

Imagining what's at the end of the tunnel. Outcome thinking removes you from your negative emotions and puts you in your desired future; it's when you re-direct and take a moment to think about the smiles on everyone's faces and the exhilarated feeling you get when you're up on stage. When you feel like you're starting to veer off on the road, engaging in negative thoughts, outcome thinking will draw you back to your target.

Robert Dilts on Creating Change

While you're trying to define your ideal outcome, take a moment to look at Robert Dilts' model and consider which areas of your life you might want to work on the most and what goals you might want to set for yourself.

Robert Dilts worked with and studied with Bandler and Grinder, the co-creators of NLP. He holds a bachelor's degree in behavioral technology from the University of California at Santa Cruz, the same university where Bandler and Grinder conducted much of the research on which NLP is based. He identified six "logical levels," areas that we identify for improvement:

1. **Spirit.** What is the larger purpose of life? Why does what you are doing matter? Schools may be concerned with educating future leaders. Maybe by becoming an athlete, you're encouraging teamwork and companionship. What is it you want to leave behind to your school, your community, or your family when you graduate? Are you sure you even *have* a sense of purpose?

2. **Identity.** Who are you? How do you want to define yourself and be defined by others?

3. **Beliefs.** What are your beliefs? Are they good ones? Or do they just keep you safe from the unknown? Are they founded on truth and kindness? Are they guided by your purpose and identity?

4. **Capabilities.** What can you do? How do you get things done? Are you a multi-tasker? Are you efficient? Or do you prefer more methodical activities?

5. **Behaviors.** How do you act? Do you act in a way that's in accordance with your identity, beliefs, and spirit?

6. **Environments.** How do external influences (friends, family, school, and peers) impact your behavior?

According to Leigh Williams Steere, co-owner of Managing People Better, Dilts' concept is this: In order to successfully enact a change, you must work at the level *above* the area you are trying to change. For example, if you want to change a behavior, then the *answer* is at a level somewhere above behavior. It might be a capability issue, a belief issue, an identity issue, or a spiritual issue. If you try to find the answer below by making an "environmental change," you'll probably experience no more than a temporary fix.

If your goal is to create change in your life, begin with an understanding of where the problem lies. Maybe you notice your friend acting like they're too good for what they're learning in class. While, let's admit it, a lot of the curriculum we learn in high school is outdated, it's important to at least try and succeed, because college is, in comparison, like the doors to heaven parting. So, knowing this, you might want to encourage your friend to stop acting like they know the world. They're disruptive in class and it only makes you look bad to sit by them. Address their behavior using the logical levels:

- **Behavior:** What behaviors are present? Your friend Sara is disruptive every afternoon and talks too much.

> - **Beliefs:** She believes that school is for "nerds."
>
> - **Capability:** Maybe you can help her improve her capabilities in reading, since she doesn't read well.
>
> - Beliefs: Find someone admirable and "cool" in the class to start talking to. Form a group with them and Sara. Now Sara has no proof that school is *just* for "nerds."
>
> - **Environment:** Change the environment to help set you guys up for success.
>
> If you had simply engaged her on the level of the problem, he or she might have been unable to come up with any solutions that addressed the underlying cause of his disruptions.

Outcome thinking encourages us to clearly define what we want so we are more likely to get it Clarity cuts through confusion and directs energy with laser focus on the desired outcome. Outcome thinking helps us shift from the problem to the process of considering solutions. Attention to the problem occupies our internal resources, making them unavailable to fully focus on the solution.

Think about the last time you were faced with a problem. Chances are you spent a lot of time and energy feeling angry, anxious, puzzled, or frustrated about the problem. You probably turned it over in your mind many times. Before you knew it, the problem seemed even larger, and you were probably emotionally exhausted. Outcome thinking focuses resources on the solution, thus changing your frame of mind from stuck to possible.

For example, suppose your friend Molly is always late to meet you whenever you hang out. She doesn't even apologize. It bugs you every time, but you don't say anything because there are a lot of different opinions about friends being late. But then after she forgets to text you to cancel and you've already waited, you decide enough is enough: it's time for a change. You start planning what you want to say to Molly and thinking about the changes you'd like to see. Now you're engaging in outcome thinking.

It is impossible to positively lead, influence, or connect with others without first building rapport. Practice using these skills until they become natural for you. Do not worry if it feels awkward at first. Remember that learning a new skill occurs in four phases: subconscious incompetence (where you do not have the skill or even an awareness of the skill deficit), conscious incompetence (an awareness of the skill deficit), conscious competence (awareness and emerging skill development), and subconscious competence (the skill is mastered and feels like second nature).

It Gets Easier!

As you work toward subconscious competence by becoming a master communicator, know that you are building the foundation for ongoing success in your personal and professional life.

As you continue to build communication skills, remember the pillars of NLP. This might take time and practice. It does not matter if you do not remember the names of each of the pillars in the beginning. What is most important is to notice how the listener is responding with words and body language to what you, the speaker, are saying. Use that information to adapt your words, voice, and body until you begin to feel rapport building.

A final note about the pillars of NLP: each is much like the tools you might use in carpentry or the kitchen. They are like your hammer and nail or your knife and salt — essential for your craft.

CASE STUDY: Helping Clients Change Behaviors and Develop New Skills with NLP

Lee McKinney
Self-empowerment hypnosis
Owner, master clinical hypnotist,
advanced NLP practitioner
seh@selfempowermenthypnosis.com
www.selfempowermenthypnosis.com

I use and have used NLP to help others make change for many years and have developed my own method of inclusion along with hypnosis, decision science and organizational behavior. My training includes membership in multiple organizations, hours of reading, seminars (including a few presented by Richard Bandler) and hands-on practice.

I have been practicing NLP for about five years, slowly incorporating it into my hypnotherapy sessions. My work with clients never excludes any issue, even ones I have never encountered previously. I truly believe that if the issue is mind-related, NLP can have a positive effect to lessen the impact of the issue and actually change the issue completely, thus improving the client's quality of life. I have worked with clients from ages five to 82. But the majority fall in the 21 to 55 age range.

Personally, I do not have a typical session. The NLP factor I use in most sessions include meta-questions to help uncover information about the client and the best way to address their issue for greater success. With that said, I do not decide on a well-formed outcome until I truly understand what is best for my client. I have seen practitioners follow training procedures so closely they almost become robotic in their actions. My focus is on customizing the experience so my client has the best possible results.

I truly believe NLP helps make physiological change to the neuro-receptors of the brain and can help set the groundwork for fast, true change and empowerment for anyone seeking self-improvement in any area.

I have found that most people know nothing about NLP or hypnosis. The people that believe they know something about NLP seem to seek an advantage in their related field of employment to improve sales turns or influence over others around them.

I incorporate NLP techniques with self-hypnosis to control pain, as well as maintain control of my emotions and not allow others to influence my feelings or actions. I have found no true measurable difference in these areas. Your life is your life, personal and professional, and you should not try to create different selves in either setting. However, you can become master of your life as a whole. NLP can help people be happier, more confident, and well-balanced as well as help them master their mental state in order to best address any situation.

The areas of change or mastery are endless. They include confidence, positive attitude, self-esteem, release from past issues, development of a new outcome from negative behaviors, greater rapport (influence) with others, self-control, improved relationship-building, memory improvement, and more.

I personally incorporate many tools to build rapport — matching, mirroring, sensory acuity, asking meta-questions, leading the conversation without dominating it, subtly agreeing with a client, and above all else, truly listening and being pleasant and easygoing with a client. I increase or decrease any of these areas according to the client. I do not believe rapport can be obtained by exclusively using any one method with all clients. You must be flexible and never set any method in stone.

I started learning and practicing hypnotherapy many years before NLP, and I see many similarities in both. NLP has a base of development from hypnosis. Though I have seen and met many NLP trainers/practitioners that have not trained in hypnosis formally and do not believe they have anything in common, I tend to agree with Richard Bandler in that both induce "trance" states, but hypnosis uses a formal induction. One way to show they have shared states is covert or conversational hypnosis, which is purely linguistic. Remember, hypnosis is 90 percent linguistically induced, but can include physical assistance to reach that state. A good hypnotherapist pays close attention to how the suggestion is given in order to greatly enhance the acceptance rate of the client at a subconscious and/or conscience level (depending on your belief of how hypnosis works). I believe the induction and the fact that many people believe that hypnosis affects only the subconscious mind are the main components that influences the pure NLP practitioner.

Speaking from my own experience, NLP is greatly intuitive. I believe one should learn all developed techniques or patterns and then incorporate them along with personal abilities/strengths as long as the result is positive. However, this only comes with time and experience. A new practitioner should gain a mastered understanding before deviating and great care must be taken when proceeding with a client. You always must be able and ready to make change to your method to meet the client's need.

If I had to choose the most important technique or pattern available from NLP, it is gaining rapport. The majority of time in my sessions it is the Milton model. I purposely take my client into a trance state before any change work is offered. I have a natural flow into the Milton model due to my hypnosis training. However, with that said, I normally utilize anchoring, reframing, Swish pattern, association/dissociation, mapping, and perceptual positions before traditional post-hypnotic suggestion. I find that the mix of the two has outstanding results. I do use the meta model to seek information from the client while gaining rapport and gain clear picture of sub-modalities. If you really dig into most NLP patterns, they all use some form of anchoring in line with sub-modalities.

I am fortunate to have hundreds of success stores. But recently I had a client, who we will call Sue, who was having a horrible time dealing with the fact that her life companion was dying from cancer. He was pushing her away during this time, and she had feelings of guilt, which in turn brought up feelings of inadequacy and abandonment, which were developed from past experiences. She was at a point of no longer going to work, getting dressed, or taking care of her personal health. She felt worthless, powerless, and undeserving of happiness. After only two sessions with both NLP and hypnosis, she was once again (according to herself and friends that came to meet me) a vivacious, confident, and happy woman. She could have empathy for her companion without the negative feelings and figured out herself that pushing her away was his way of trying to protect her from the results of this horrible ordeal. We were also successful in placing the old experiences in her "mental library" to be used as reference to help protect her from reliving the same issues in her present and future life, preventing these negative experiences to impact her emotions or actions again.

Anyone seeking change in any aspect can improve his or her quality of life personally or professionally with NLP. I would say if you get the opportunity to learn from the creator of the method or someone trained by him or her that would be your best bet. With that said, anyone can learn and apply the principles, but it does take practice to master.

Bandler's or Grinder's books and seminars seem to dominate the NLP training scene, and there is a lot of information on the web. But beware — a lot of trash appears there as well. If you can, joining a group with others who are interested in learning and or practicing NLP is a good place to start.

Science does not support a multitude of subjects and practices. That does not mean they do not work or are not real. The simple answer is that I can prove it works to help a person change a belief or behavior because I have seen positive results with my clients. The opportunities are endless for NLP and hypnosis to have a powerful and positive impact in our world today to help us all lead a better quality of life. Above all else, you can never allow others to set their limitations on you.

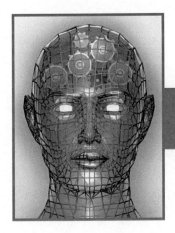

CHAPTER 5

Focus on the Outcome Frame

The first four chapters of this book mainly covered the "what" of NLP, and the rest of the book will cover the "how." By taking notes and participating in the exercises, you are already mastering the art of NLP. Continue on, and you will be a true guru. This chapter focuses on how you will create an incredibly well-defined outcome frame.

Sometimes the goals we set are simple and easy to achieve. For example, a goal might be to read one book each month. Other goals are more complex, like learning to speak another language. No matter the goal, a focus on the outcome frame offers a more nuanced way of thinking about and approaching the goal. The outcome frame brings a complete picture, including the feelings involved, of completing the goal into clear focus.

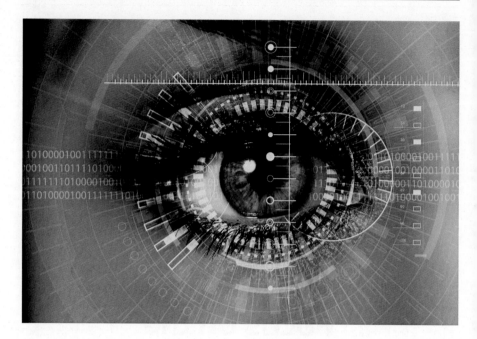

Your focus on the outcome frame is much like blueprints are to a house. Well-designed blueprints improve the chances for a well-built house. They also provide an opportunity to create a visual representation of the physical house. In other words, you see the house before it becomes real. Trying to reach a goal without an outcome frame is like building a house without a blueprint: it will most likely crumble and fall!

Outcome Frame Defined

In the simplest terms, an outcome is a developed goal, desire, or dream. Our previous example of learning to speak another language articulates a desire or goal; it does not consider how the goal can be achieved. The outcome frame does just that — as long as it meets the five following conditions.

1. **The goal must be stated in positive terms**. In other words, the goal should identify what you want or value. According to Dr.

Norman Vincent Peale, author of *The Power of Positive Thinking*, positive thinking leads to confidence, success, and achievement. Positive thinking is at the heart of NLP, and it's the engine you need to realize your dreams.

> *Example:* "I want to learn to speak another language." This goal is stated in positive terms.

The goal should not state what you do not want.

> *Example:* "I do not want to feel like an idiot when I travel abroad without speaking the language." This goal is stated in negative terms.

There is an advantage to stating a goal in positive terms. Stating something in the negative suggests that you have to "get through" something. The idea of getting through something can feel draining and use energy that could be better put toward the accomplishment. Stating something in the positive suggests that you "can do" something. Feeling that you can do something is empowering and energy producing. That energy can be used to toward accomplishing your outcome.

2. **The goal must be sensory-based.** A sensory-based goal connects you to the outcome by allowing you to use your senses to describe how it feels to achieve what you want. Using your senses to experience your goal engages your subconscious mind in support of the outcome. When your subconscious mind embraces the outcome, feelings of resistance, and the resulting self-sabotage, are greatly reduced or eliminated.

> *Example:* Envision yourself traveling on the train in the country you will be visiting. Feel the delight of enjoying

the casual conversations you hear. Or, see yourself confidently asking about good places to visit for dinner. Feel how good it is to know what to say.

The mind and body are related and do not operate independently of one another. Sensory-based goals align bodies with our minds in support of that goal. It is impossible to achieve any goal without cooperation from both.

3. **The goal must be one that you value and can control**. Your interest in achieving the goal must come from your unique personal motivation or mission. Your personal mission speaks to larger life questions such as who you are or want to be. The goal should not be one you only think you should achieve based on the people, fads, or pressures around you. Why do you want to waste all your time and energy saving up for the new iPhone coming out in the fall? If you had an honest conversation with yourself, would you really think this desire for the iPhone arose from *deep within you?* Think closer to "What is my life's purpose?" and farther away from "What is the next thing that I'll buy that I'll throw away in a year?"

> *Example:* "I want to learn Chinese because it is a popular language right now." The goal is properly stated in positive terms, but it does not meet the conditions for an outcome because it does not identify a personal motivation for achieving the goal. The example goal as stated would only be useful if the motivation is to be and do what is popular.

> *Example:* "I want to learn Chinese because I plan to live in China for a year to study." The goal is properly stated

in positive terms, and it identifies a personal motivation (being prepared to study in China) for accomplishment.

You should also be able to rely exclusively, or almost exclusively, on your own actions to achieve your goal. In other words, achieving the goal should be within your control. Can you teach your dog Chinese? No. Can you take on other people's goals for them? No. Can you make other people think certain things about you? No. Your goal must be within *your control.*

> *Example:* "Actions I can take to achieve my goal of learning Chinese include: enrolling in a class, hiring a tutor, buying and studying language tapes, and using a language learning computer software program, DVD, or podcast." You can also set up a study schedule and make a calendar to be sure that you do not schedule events that conflict with your lessons.

4. **The goal should have a context.** You can contextualize your goal by asking questions that clarify the circumstances of the outcome. Providing context for your goal is much like giving the goal an anchor in reality (so it doesn't hover away!).

   Example:

   - **When** will you know you have accomplished your goal? My goal of learning another language will be accomplished **when** I can confidently converse in that language. My goal of learning another language will be accomplished **when** I can read a Chinese newspaper or understand Chinese radio.

   - **Who** and **where** questions are also helpful for contextualizing a goal. For example, **who** will be a part of celebrating, supporting, or benefiting from your goal? **Who** will be present as you accomplish your goal? Do not be shy about naming the specific people who will be involved. For example, **who** will be in your study group? **How** will you celebrate, and with **whom**, once the goal has been accomplished? Remember, you want to have the internal experience of the accomplishment, as vividly as possible, when you are planning for a successful outcome.

   - **Where** will you derive the most benefit from your achievement? (Will the accomplishment be most helpful in your personal or academic life?) **Where** will you work toward your achievement (on a practical level, you should know where in your home you will be able to concentrate while you study)?

5. **The goal should fit your individual values, needs, and interests.** Your goals are as personal as, well, *you*. Your goals in life define you, no matter how big or small they are. Maybe your goal in life is to live simply. That's great! It suits *you*. And that's what matters. The goal should never be at odds with the values, needs, and interests that you hold dear to yourself.

Evaluating needs, values, and interests early can eliminate obstacles and pitfalls later on. This information can help you develop a workable plan that you are less likely to abandon. For example, what resources do you already have in place? What resources do you need? Here you will want to consider material resources (such as a DVD player) and internal resources (such as skills, knowledge, and confidence).

Recall the presupposition, "People have all the resources they need." Name all the resources you can think of that you will need to meet your outcome. Begin with internal resources. You will be able to access the resources you need even if you do not feel immediately connected to them.

Internal Resources for Achieving Outcomes

Learning another language might require confidence. Confidence is an example of an internal resource. Try to think of another time you needed confidence to accomplish something that felt very big. Maybe you were asking someone cute out on a date. Maybe you were doing a debate in front of your entire school. Often, the more dramatic and risky the situation is, the more fearful we feel. And we need confidence to build a momentum and come out on top.

So, even if you are not feeling very confident when you begin learning Chinese, you might use an anchor to bring about a state of confidence each time you begin a lesson. We will discuss anchoring more in-depth in Chapter 7. Triggering an anchor can help you move from a non-useful state (such as lacking confidence) to a useful one (like feeling confident in your ability to learn Chinese).

Discipline or staying on task can also be an internal resource. If you find it difficult to study when your favorite program is on television, it will be important to decide whether you are appropriately motivated to achieve your outcome. If you have checked your motivation and found that it answers a question or need that comes from within, you might simply need a quick run through of the Godiva Chocolate pattern exercise to stay on track. (See Chapter 3, exercise 5 for more information on this pattern.)

Material or External Resources for Achieving Outcomes

You will also need to consider what material resources are available to you in support of your goal. If you choose a study group or class, you will need to consider how you will get to those meetings. For example, do you have the money for public transit? Can you carpool to the class, or is it feasible to start a study group at work or school? As much as we'd like to say that your fingertips are magic and everything you touch will turn into dream sparkles, this is simply not the case. There are practical considerations that you must consider, even more so if you're dependent on your parents for income.

Each of the five conditions of an outcome frame is important for achieving a goal by first developing that goal into an outcome. In terms of prioritizing the conditions, the first condition — *State the goal in positive terms* — is perhaps the most important. Nothing else you do toward achieving the outcome will matter if you do not believe the outcome is possible for you.

Turn your goals into accomplishments by exploring them with the five conditions in mind. As you begin, consider using a journal to write down your plans and chart your progress. You might also consider talking with friends or family members to be sure you have not overlooked an obstacle or resource. Be clear about your motivations. Finally, remember to circle dates on a calendar you see regularly and include dates by each of the steps that lead you to your goal. Your success will be inevitable.

CASE STUDY:
Life Transformations
with NLP

Jaime Rojas
Certified Life Coach though the
society of NLP as a master coach
www.positivelystrong.com

I was introduced to NLP by Tony Robbins about six years ago. I have been certified for five years and deal with an average of five clients each day. My experience has been fantastic in the sense that the changes are huge and often happen in a matter of minutes. However, I have noticed some aspects of peeling the onion, if you will, that sometimes require additional work.

For example, the minute my clients have gotten down to the root of their issue, their uncertainty sometimes becomes higher because they realize that they are in the wrong career or have chosen the wrong spouse. At this point, they have made agreements with themselves and others that they do not believe they can break. Breaking those agreements can be the toughest thing to do.

I had a client that I will call Maria. She came to me because she felt that she needed a motivation anchor. Maria had wanted to break the record of paddling a surfboard from Cuba to the coast of Florida, a 90-mile trip in shark-infested waters. That is some accomplishment, right?

I began by talking with her to understand her world and how it was represented for her. Maria was born into a very religious family. She had been feeling very insignificant lately because she had just found the courage to tell her mother that she was gay. Her mother rejected her and kicked her out of her home. Accomplishing this feat was significant, even if it would cost her life, because she had convinced herself and other people around her that she was doing it for charity purposes. In reality, she created this goal to meet her need for significance, especially in her mother's eyes.

I have had the privilege of working with children as young as six years old, a 21-year-old who had been feeling suicidal, and even a 60-year-old. NLP is effective across age groups. The techniques make it is so easy to establish rapport, which you can do in literally five minutes. A typical session involves stepping into my client's world to connect with them every time. Of course, listening is key to building a relationship and dealing with the particular issue of the day.

The pattern that I have found so far is that it takes anywhere from one to 12 sessions to make radical changes in behavior. I especially enjoy hearing from clients months later who thank me and let me know how much better they feel. This work is very fulfilling. Usually, people are thinking, "Just help me deal with this issue," when in reality they do not know what the real issue is.

I feel that the benefit of NLP is the ability to create the game of life in a winnable way. NLP allows my clients to get rid of all those fears that were learned and to reconnect with that spiritual aspect of themselves. That is why I use these strategies every day in my own life with family members and friends.

Back to Maria the athlete. We worked together to change the meaning, or representation, that life was only about achievement to the idea that life was a playground. I believe that anyone can use these skills to influence themselves and then other people. That is why I recommend people investigate NLP to learn how it can help them create the changes they really want.

Exercise 6:
Fun Uses for NLP

"Will It Sell? Filters for Nonfiction Submissions"

Used with permission from Leigh Steere

Confession: I am not a publisher or an author. Instead, I am a bookworm with a background in neuro-linguistics, which explores the relationship between language and attention.

At any given moment, my nightstand is cluttered with a wide array of books. Right now? *Animorphs #20, Peacemaker Student Edition, Outliers*, a Star Wars early reader on podracing, Three Cups of Tea, a book on menopause, and one on management. Eclectic, eh? (I have three kids.)

I am fairly patient, and I am willing to plow through less-than-engaging tomes to extract pearls of wisdom from experts. But my patience has a limit. If I start drifting off in the middle of a page (and if that happens several times), I have a rule. I stop reading and donate the book to the library fundraising shelf. Some other poor soul might have the same dry reading experience, but at least the library will be a dollar richer.

We live in a time-strapped culture where we carefully weigh how to use our precious moments of free time. "Entertainment value" has become a major selection criterion for how we spend our money and time off — and for how we select nonfiction books.

Out of curiosity, and because of my neuro-linguistics training, I recently examined some yawner books to determine why they were not engaging. In the process, I found two filters that publishers can use in selecting and editing nonfiction manuscripts.

Test for Spinout

Definition: "Spinout" occurs when a reader mentally leaves the text to process information and then does not return to finish reading the text.

Technical explanation: Neuro-linguistic practitioners teach a technique for listening and coaching that involves using non-sensory specific language to ask questions or invite people to consider new information. For example, a listener might ask:

- What do you think should happen next?
- What do you recommend?
- What thoughts come to mind when you consider this information?

These sample questions do not contain strongly visual, auditory, or kinesthetic language. They are sensory-generic and invite the responder to access all representation systems in formulating an answer. As a result:

- The listener usually gets a richer response.
- The responder sometimes gets lost in rich thought.

In one-on-one settings, if responders get lost in thought, listeners can pull them back to the conversation with a follow-up question, such as: "You seem to be processing something. Can you share what's on your mind?"

But what happens if a sensory-generic question or statement in a book prompts the reader to get lost in rich thought? Sometimes, the reader does not return to the text.

Example: "Both overuse their natural style and become less effective."

Diagnosis: This sentence is concise, clear, and technically perfect. But, can you make a picture of what this means in your mind? Or can you imagine how it sounds or feels? No. It is sensory-generic and poses a risk for spinout.

When readers spin out, those who do not absolutely need the information in a book may set the book aside. These readers might conclude — consciously or unconsciously — that the book is taking too long to read, and they might opt for another book or activity. They might decide the book is "dry" and not recommend it to others.

Rx: If you find yourself spinning out while reading a non-fiction manuscript, look carefully at the language. If it is sensory-generic, you can determine how much effort will be required to infuse visual, auditory, and kinesthetic language. By shifting the balance between types of illustrations and language, you may be able to increase the book's chances of success.

By the way, you probably spun out a little bit while reading this section. How did it feel?

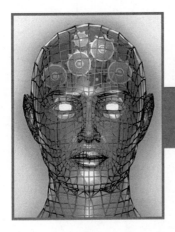

CHAPTER 6

Understanding Communication

P oor communication will always present problems. Recall the presuppositions, "You cannot not communicate" and "The meaning of communication is the response you get." Communication encompasses so much more than the words we speak. What is important to remember about communication is that we are always communicating or transmitting messages. And if we want to be effective communicators, we will make sure to get our desired response.

We know that communication happens when we interact with others. There is another way of communicating that we do not often think about. In addition to communicating with others, we communicate with ourselves. There is an almost constant dialogue taking place between mind and body, or even different parts of our mind to others. That dialogue guides our thoughts, feelings, decisions, and actions.

This chapter is dedicated entirely to communication and how it takes place within ourselves and between us and other people.

How Do We Communicate?

One of the ways we communicate is through representational systems. In NLP, these are called "sense modalities." Your representational, or "rep system," helps you recognize the information that comes in through your senses. These senses vary from your sight, hearing, sense of smell, and touch. You use this information in many ways — even when you don't know it! Subtle messages from your environment will often be detected by your senses and guide you in unexpected ways.

Representational systems help us store and recall information. Think of a vivid experience. Chances are that you recalled the experience through the senses that originally helped you define that experience. If your memory is a county fair, for example, you might remember what a beautiful day it was; you might remember the feeling of the warm sun, see the vibrant blue sky or fluffy white clouds, hear children laughing, or smell popcorn. Your representational system helps you take in, interpret, store, and recall all the information or messages around you.

The power of NLP is in its encouragement to use representational systems to also create experiences. By using the power of our senses, we can create an experience in our minds that we would like to have in our lives. The idea here is to use your representational system to create an experience that feels so real, it becomes almost like a memory or something that has already happened. As the experience becomes more real, any resistance to achieving it is lessened and motivation to achieve it grows. By making a dream real and tangible, it feels less like an imagined thing and more like one you can touch, smell, and hold.

As you use your senses to create new experiences for yourself, make sure to use *many of them at a time.* Using all or most of your senses generally produces a very strong response and leads to higher motivation. Using only one or two senses will produce a weaker response and is not likely to facilitate high motivation to achieve the experience.

You will learn even more about tracking representational systems in communication with others as you learn about predicates in the following section.

Predicates

NLP uses the word *predicates* to describe the clues that reveal the representational system being used. Predicates can be verbal or non-verbal. Verbal predicates include terms such as "I hear," "I feel," or "I see." Nonverbal predicates include gestures or body language. These non-verbal clues also offer valuable information that reveals what is thought or felt. Watch and listen for predicates to understand the representational system being used.

The next time you are engaged in conversation, watch and listen to notice the primary representational system (PRS) being used. For example, someone with a visual PRS might talk about a vacation using words that describe what he or she saw, such as "the lush green trees," while another person with an auditory PRS might remember the sound of the ocean or the crickets at night.

Most of us use all representational systems with one system being more dominant than the others. Another way to look for the PRS being used is to notice non-verbal predicates. In our vacation example, the speaker describing his or her vacation with visual words might first look up while accessing the words. The person with the auditory primary representational system might begin by looking to the side.

CASE STUDY: Predicates to Communicate with Yourself

You can use predicates to improve communication with people by detecting their preferences. Are they more visual? Speak to them in visual terms and use hand gestures and descriptive language. Are they more auditory? Speak in a clear and articulate way, put some melody and pep in your voice. If you really want to go to the movies, and your dad is a visual person, make sure to throw in a word about the "stunning cinematography" or how beautiful the lead actress is. In determining these preferences, you will improve your overall experience for everyone.

So, how can you use predicates to communicate with yourself? Now that you've determined some goals for yourself, you'll want to use predicates to make them real for you. Make sure to imagine what your goals would feel, look, and sound like. By taking five or 10 minutes to devote to each sense, you will make this experience real and it will feel that much more achievable!

How can predicates improve communication?

Predicates tell us something about the dominant sense being used by the other person to understand information. One of the primary goals of successful communication is building rapport. Rapport is basically a feeling of trust. When you show that you are listening to a person, they will like you better (so remember that when your teacher is chastising you for not doing your homework!). Identifying the representational system being used by listening for and matching the predicate is an easy way to build rapport.

For example, you can match predicates with someone that demonstrates an auditory sense mode by leaning your ear in close while he or she is speaking and by using words that conjure up strong sounds. Use words that create an image when you want to match predicates with a visual person. Matching predicates suggests to the other person that you understand their feelings and motivations, thus creating feelings of trust and rapport.

Eye-accessing cues

The next time you talk with someone, watch his or her eyes. Almost everyone unconsciously moves his or her eyes while talking and listening. This eye movement is an external sign that information is being considered or processed internally. Watching how the eyes move is a clue to how the information is being processed. NLP calls these techniques eye-accessing cues. The movement and direction of the eyes tells whether someone is hearing or seeing images, or even experiencing feelings internally.

A lot has changed in the science of face reading and eye tracking. Generally, though, if people look up and to the right, they are using their visual imagination. If people look up and to the left, they are using their auditory senses. Take a moment to look over psychological literature on face reading so you can detect their dominant predicates.

Exercise 7:
Using NLP to Improve
Conversational Outcomes

All of us have had the experience of talking with someone who was difficult. I mean, just think about the last conversation with your parents. Use the following steps to improve conversational outcomes even with the most challenging people in your life.

Step 1: Determine the outcome. Begin by spending a few moments to clarify what you hope to achieve with the conversation. In other words, what do you want the outcome to be? Do you want agreement or cooperation? Are you hoping the other person will see your point of view? Agree to let you go to a summer program? Agree to go to this place for food instead of that one? Be clear about your outcome, which is much like a destination. You must know where you want to go so you will know when you have accomplished what you set out to do at the start of the conversation. Just remember, it's okay if this outcome is not achieved (other people have their own preferences and desires, too). It's just best to know what you want so you don't get derailed and sidetracked.

Step 2: Decide on plan B. Consider the need for a plan B. For this example, we will assume you are trying to get your date to agree to a late evening dinner instead of an afternoon lunch, since it's more romantic. Plan B will be the difference between the best-case scenario and the good-enough scenario. An example of these scenarios might be the following:

Best case: You do exactly what you want: a late evening stroll in the park and dinner at your favorite Thai restaurant.

Good enough: You guys go in the early evening and eat dinner.

It can also be useful to consider a plan C. Do you abandon the whole thing if you cannot get to your desired conversational outcome? Absolutely not. This is a perfect opportunity to reframe. Maybe the person you're asking out isn't completely comfortable with evening dates yet. Maybe they're shy. Maybe they have a specific evening routine with their family. It is important to reposition yourself when it comes down to "all or nothing." Do you really want to walk away completely empty handed?

Step 3: Determine which emotional state you need to be successful. Choose your most resourceful emotional state. How will you need to feel and what will you need to think as you begin and continue the conversation? If you are talking with a particularly difficult person, it will probably be important to feel calm and patient. If you are talking with an angry or aggressive person, you might want to appear confident. And if you are talking with someone that has doubts about what you are saying, you might want to come across as knowledgeable and reassuring. Remember that you can easily access the desired state by firing an anchor to trigger that state. Take a few moments to visualize yourself having the conversation in your desired state. See the body language you will use, your words, as well as your tone of voice.

Step 4: Look for clues to build rapport. Remember to continue building rapport as you converse. Respond to the PRS (preferred representational system) of the person you are talking with. You should also understand something about how she or he is motivated — "toward" or "away from". Someone with a "toward" motivation takes action to gain something or with a payoff in mind. This kind of person wants to get to work early because he or she likes to enjoy a relaxing cup of coffee before beginning the work day. An individual with an "away from" motivation takes action to avoid something. This person gets to work early because he or she does not want to be fired.

Step 5: Consider the second perceptual position. Adopt the other person's point of view or perceptual position. What is he or she thinking and feeling about what is being communicated?

Step 6: Acknowledge areas of agreement. Look for and point to any areas of general agreement to build on. Maybe you and your potential date agree that you absolutely love arcades. Maybe it's better to suggest a nerdy-gaming date as opposed to a movie-screen one!

Step 7: Clarify and wrap-up the discussion. Recall the presupposition, "You cannot not communicate." Communication is at the heart of every relationship, even the most casual or fleeting ones such as between you and the cashier at your local grocery store. Both of you will take something away from that exchange based on what you see and hear. The value of understanding communication is at least two-fold.

Firstly, you can decide the kind of messages you want to communicate. And secondly, you can practice the skills you need to communicate intended messages across a variety of settings. Communicating unintended messages results in conflict and misunderstanding. Before anyone else can know what you're saying, *you* have to know what you're saying! This is a lot more difficult than it sounds. Maybe you're having a difficult day because you were rejected by someone. So you start saying mean and hurtful things without knowing it to others. In this case, you want to boost up your awareness so you can communicate in a way that better suits your goals.

CASE STUDY:
The Benefits of NLP

Leigh Steere
Incisive B2B and
Managing People Better, LLC
Owner of Incisive;
Co-owner of Managing People Better, LLC
www.managingpeoplebetter.com

I have been practicing NLP since January 1994. Professionally, I have used NLP in:

- Coaching employees on job performance issues
- Providing career counseling
- Interviewing prospective new hires
- Solving complex conflicts
- Branding projects (to influence employee and consumer behavior)
- Analyzing messages (helping employers understand what messages employees received vs. what messages the employers intended)
- Designing curriculum for hard- and soft-skills training

I use NLP to help inspire attitude and behavior shifts — and to help others understand the dynamics of what is happening when they are not getting the behaviors or attitudes they want. I also use NLP to help people understand each other's communication style and preferences.

NLP provides a comprehensive framework for understanding human communication and behavior. If I am not getting the result I want, I have a tool kit for understanding why and for formulating alternative communication approaches.

I think most people really do not know what to expect. They often sign up for an NLP class based on the recommendation of an enthusiastic friend who is evangelizing the merits of NLP. They know their friend is excited and they trust their friend's opinions. They become curious enough to spend the time and money to find out more. I believe many people look at NLP as an adventure into the unknown. They sign up as a leap of faith.

I use NLP every day. It is such an integrated part of how I think that I no longer consciously say, "What can I use from NLP for this situation?" In my opinion, it is an essential tool kit for self-examination and for effective communication, negotiation, and conflict resolution at home and at work. NLP is equally effective in both personal and professional settings.

Rapport happens on many levels. It starts when we mirror body language and listen and watch to understand whether a person leads with the visual, auditory, or kinesthetic representation systems (or occasionally, gustatory or olfactory). As we start communicating with a person through their leading representation system, rapport deepens. If we listen for metaprograms such as "toward" or "away from" thinking, we can further deepen rapport by acknowledging through our own communication that we understand where the person is coming from.

To use non-NLP parlance, rapport is about stepping into someone else's shoes and seeing, hearing, or feeling the world from their perspective. Most people tend to look through their own "lens" or "filters." NLP helps you develop the flexibility to experience the world through someone else's glasses. When we have the ability to do this, we can see the root of a conflict. We can understand how to communicate in a way the audience will actually "hear" — in a way that helps our message come across as intended.

I use both the meta model and the Milton model. I do not consciously think about a distinction between the two.

I think it is helpful to understand if there is a current anchor holding a limiting belief or behavior in place. I do not consciously think about anchoring in my work, but I suppose I am helping to create new anchors through many of the communication projects I work on. If you are trying to help a person shift from behavior/attitude A to behavior/attitude B, then the process is much like a boat. You need to lift the anchor and reel it in before you can move to the next destination.

Once you get to the new destination, you drop anchor to hold your position. If a boat does not lift its anchor, the anchor drags along the bottom, gets caught on things, and impedes progress and speed. The concept of anchoring is critical to NLP. Many therapists, corporate coaches, and corporate communicators inadvertently try to create change while an anchor is dragging the bottom of the waterway.

I use NLP to create new "frameworks" for helping people get their arms around complex problems. Any adult — and even teenagers — can benefit from NLP. It is vital to engage all sensory systems in learning NLP. In a well-run training, the instructors are using all modalities to teach and demonstrate nuances. They are explaining the concepts, providing visual demonstrations, having you practice bodily, and providing detailed visual, auditory, and kinesthetic feedback to help you fine tune your approach. There are some concepts that a person could learn from a book and apply without further training, but a person can apply the concepts even better with in-person, highly interactive instruction.

As an example, in my practitioner training, I was paired for an exercise with a woman who had really struggled with interpersonal relationships. She was very isolated and could not figure out what to do differently. She had enrolled in the NLP class, hoping for communication skills that would help her in relationship building.

As part of the exercise, I needed to determine her leading representation system. I was looking, listening, and feeling for visual, auditory, and kinesthetic because that is what we had been focusing on in class. Part way through the exercise, it dawned on me. She was leading with the olfactory system — exceedingly rare for someone born and raised in the United States. Her sweetest memories were stored in her sense of smell. There is no way a book could impart the impact I experienced in this exercise. I was awash in a sense of grief for this person, as it became painfully clear why she was having trouble maintaining rapport with people.

I recommend NLP Comprehensive in Colorado, particularly its summer immersion trainings. People from all continents attend these intensive sessions, so you get the cross-cultural experience in addition to the NLP learning.

In reply to the "not supported by science" assertions, I ask, "What do you mean by that?" Usually, I find people who say this are basing their statement on something they have heard from others. They have not really researched the question themselves. Their statements come from a place of misunderstanding. And that's not really effective communication in the first place, is it?

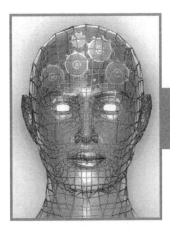

CHAPTER 7

Metaprograms

The word metaprogram sounds complicated and mysterious, but it is actually very easy to understand. In the simplest terms, a metaprogram is like an internal instruction manual we use to create thoughts and take actions. The word metaprogram comes from the influence of something called cybernetics on the field of NLP (we won't go into any further detail on this).

Each of us uses rules or metaprograms that tell us what to do with and how to respond to the information we take in. Metaprograms form the foundation of our mental processes. Metaprograms explain why two people might arrive at different conclusions from the same information.

Consider the following example: Susan and Lucy attend a ceramics class where the instructor describes and demonstrates several kinds of pottery. Susan takes in each description and demonstration. She feels excited about the ceramic jar she plans on making. Lucy, however, has a different experience. In fact, Lucy feels so overwhelmed by the possibilities that she is unable to make a choice at all. Her mind is, whether she is aware of it or not, interpreting the information in a way that makes it more difficult for her to decide. In this example, both Susan and Lucy "see" what is possible, but each has different rules or metaprograms for how to think about and respond to so many choices.

Metaprograms are to people what software programs are to computers. The programs use a set of rules to analyze data and drive actions. Remember the discussion about "away from" vs. "toward" motivation direction? The "toward" or "away from" motivation direction is a strategy one chooses based on the information as processed in the metaprogram.

Understanding your metaprograms and creating new, more enlightened and productive ones will be the focus of this chapter.

Mental Processes

Your subconscious mind is always taking in and sending out information. The subconscious mind stores everything we are not consciously aware of. Some kinds of information, such as background noise, moves easily from our subconscious to our conscious minds; other information does not surface in our conscious awareness. Sometimes, we only know this information is there because of how it shows up in our behavior or decisions.

For example, we may realize a certain friend makes us feel uncomfortable because they're always undercutting or teasing you passive aggressively. How we *interpret* this information is up to our metaprograms. We may notice ourselves hunching over or being silent around this friend, and our metaprogram may tell us that we *should* be ashamed and act accordingly, sulking, not responding, agreeing for the sake of reducing conflict.

In other words, our metaprograms and their interpretations are important to be cognizant of, especially if we've adopted maladaptive ones.

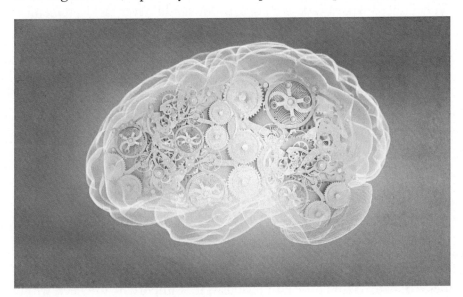

Filters that Determine How the World is Viewed

We are always taking in information. We take in so much that it cannot all be stored in our conscious mind. Much of the information we take in is filtered — we keep some and discard some, or compact or generalize it using it as a short hand of sorts. We also distort some of the information we take in. What we do with this information will depend on language, beliefs, and decisions which are our "metaprograms." For example, if someone pays you a compliment that you do not agree with, such as "You are pretty," you may choose to discard that information because you do not believe it. And what a waste, isn't it?

Working with limiting beliefs

Sometimes our own thoughts and beliefs stand between our present state and our desired state. For example, you may want to complete a marathon, but you don't think you can really do it. One of the easiest ways to work with limiting beliefs is to look for evidence to the contrary. When faced with a task you are sure you could never tackle, remember another time you tackled a seemingly impossible task. Ask someone to help you list objective facts, because in some cases your beliefs may cause you to deny the evidence even as you present it to yourself! For instance, this person might point out sports competitions you won, or even a time when you stepped out of your comfort zone and became really good at something you didn't expect.

In his book, *Beliefs: Pathways to Health & Well-Being*, Robert Dilts has distilled the process of change into one simple formula that essentially describes every NLP strategy. Take the present state (the state where you are currently experiencing the problem) and add resources to arrive at your desired state. As mentioned previously, it is important to check within yourself for resistance, or what Dilts called interference. As you dig deeper and unearth metaprograms you never knew you had, built-in software you'd never even seen before, you will meet resistance. Your metaprograms really are your everything: beliefs, values, and methods of interpretation that have been running your life. It's easy to see why questioning them is so difficult. But they are the very things that may be holding you back.

As you work to change them, you will likely meet some internal objection, usually one of three types.

Common Factors in Resistance to Change

Creating change is about more than making a decision and buckling up. The process of change is complex and involves the relationship between mind, body, and the social systems — such as family and faith community — around you. When you meet resistance on your way to change, take time to identify the resistance so you can plan a way to around it. The following are some common things that contribute to our resistance to change:

- **Reward**: A reward for resisting the change is the most common. For example, Denis wants to quit smoking marijuana with his friends, but that's the only time they all hang out and see each other. Although he understands the benefits of what's becoming a bad habit, he would also miss the time spent with his friends.

- **Lack of Knowledge**: Another type of interference involves lack of knowledge. You might want to make a change but you do not know how to go about it. For example, you might have some great ideas for a new dress, but before you can make it you will have to learn how to sew. You feel completely in the dark and a little overwhelmed with a lack of resources.

- **Insufficient Time**: Finally, you might become discouraged before you even make the change because you have not given yourself the chance or enough time to make the change. Say you want to learn to play the guitar. You take lessons for a month and become discouraged that you are not yet comfortable with the chords. This is not a realistic expectation to have after just a few days. Since everything is so quick with technology now, it's hard to realize that real life goes at a much slower pace. It takes time and true commitment to learn or do anything.

How to Use Metaprograms in NLP

Everyone has his or her own style of motivation. Understanding metaprograms helps you motivate others as well as find your own motivation. Identifying metaprograms can also help you build rapport with others.

There are seven common programs that most people employ to some degree. NLP researchers have determined that people often use the same metaprogram under a variety of circumstances.

"Toward" vs. "away from"

We have discussed this metaprogram previously. "Toward" vs. "away from" describes a common motivation strategy or metaprogram. As you will recall, individuals motivated in a "toward" direction will take action in anticipation of a reward. Individuals motivated in an "away from" direction will take action to avoid a negative consequence. Both directions have benefits and drawbacks. Although most people using this metaprogram use both directions, they will often be more motivated in one direction than the other.

Proactive vs. reactive

Proactive people are more likely to jump in first and consider later; these kinds of people are initiators. Reactive people are responders; they consider what is happening before jumping in. Again, both programs have advantages. In the classroom, proactive students are likely the ones that sign up to plan and organize the first annual fall harvest carnival. Reactive students would likely respond to requests for carnival volunteers. Understanding individual motivation style helps you tailor your approach to fit the metaprogram.

Sameness vs. difference

In this category, people are motivated by creating change or difference or maintaining things as they are. People with a sameness metaprogram value constancy. They like to create situations that feel familiar. Sameness should not imply that these people do not like change at all; they are likely to accept gradual changes. People motivated by difference are driven to create change.

Internal vs. external

People with an internal motivation filter ideas, values, and standards through their own individual standards. As you might expect, people with external motivation derive their feedback from external sources. Parents of children with a meta program that values external motivation should offer a lot of praise and positive feedback to reinforce desired behaviors.

Options vs. procedures

The difference here is between actively seeking options and acting by the book. The short definition of this program might sound like the difference between possibility and process. The options person is excited and motivated by all the possible ways to look at and approach a given situation. Conversely, the procedures person uses processes or rules to decide how to approach a given situation. Government workers are often stereotypically described as procedure-oriented. Conversely, teenagers and young adults are often thought of as options-oriented; they often buck procedures and look for ways to blaze a new path.

Global vs. detail

Like the word suggests, people who operate from global metaprograms prefer the big picture. These kinds of people look for the overall view and work from there, believing the details can be filled in once the general overview has been established. The opposite kind of metaprogram, detail, is motivated by smaller bits of information. Here, it is the specifics of the situation that matter, along with the belief that the big picture will take care of itself after the details have been addressed.

Introvert vs. extrovert

You have most likely heard these words before to describe personality types. The terms have a slightly different connotation with NLP, where the focus is not on the difference between having a shy or outgoing personality. Instead, the focus is on how your metaprogram leads you to restore your emotional energy. People who operate from an introvert metaprogram typically feel restored by alone time. These kinds of people recover from stress and other difficult emotions by spending restorative, quiet time with themselves. Extroverts find their energy in the company of others. In fact, unlike introverts, extroverts often find large groups of people to be energizing rather than draining.

Identifying Metaprograms

Metaprograms govern much about how we approach any tasks. You can identify your metaprogram simply by noticing patterns in your own behavior and thoughts. For example, if you exercise regularly because you love the energetic way it makes you feel, you are using a toward motivation. If, on the other hand, you exercise regularly because you do not want to gain weight, you are operating from an away from motivation. Look at each of the metaprograms listed above to understand your motivation style.

You can also listen to others to understand how they are motivated. Casual questions often reveal a great deal when you understand metaprograms. For example, simply asking someone why he or she chose their career field or what he or she like about the job can reveal a lot of information. Someone that says she went into her chosen field because she really enjoys the dynamic environment and appreciates that she never knows what to expect from one day to the next might be operating on the difference spectrum of the same vs. difference metaprogram.

Remember, metaprograms can come in these general orientations such as those outlined above, but they can also be very general beliefs about how you fit into the world. Let's say you have a very deep-rooted belief in yourself that you're just "not good enough." This is a very strong belief that will filter information in specific ways. For instance, when you're rejected by a certain group of people at school, you may forget about the times when you had fun with your other groups of friends and feel like a social failure. Your beliefs and values are very much a part of your metaprogram software, so to speak, as well as your different orientations and preferences.

Although it was previously believed that metaprograms were fixed and could not be changed, it is now known based on research by Robert Dilts, a leading thinker in NLP, that this is not the case. Although there are advantages and disadvantages to each kind of metaprogram, individuals wishing to change metaprograms that feel limiting can do so. A simple strategy for doing this follows.

Exercise 8: Changing Metaprograms

Metaprograms guide decisions about which perceptions will be highlighted for attention and subsequent action. If the metaprogram you are using leads you to a focus that is not useful, you can change it.

Step 1: Target the metaprogram you want to change. In what context do you use this program? Why do you think it does not work for you? Here is an example: Carla is a big-picture or global thinker. She is not concerned with details, which bore her. In history class, she can never remember specific details. She's always forgetting the "little things" that make a huge difference. Although this metaprogram works well when she's brainstorming, it does not work during the execution of her ideas.

Step 2: Identify the more helpful metaprogram. Carla needs to be able to fill in the big picture or get a more detailed understanding of things.

Step 3: Understand why the new metaprogram is needed. Carla's motivation for making the change from a global metaprogram to a detail metaprogram may be based on her need to succeed in school and be more well rounded.

Step 4: Practice the new metaprogram. As you shift programs in your mind, move your physical position. For example, stand in another part of the room or sit in a different chair. Carla should visualize the experience of providing details. How does the new metaprogram look and feel? Associate with this feeling as if it is happening in the moment. How does this new metaprogram fit with or change your identity?

Step 5: Check within for resistance or interference with your conscious goal of changing your metaprogram. Is there any part of you that receives some benefit or reward from using the old metaprogram? Is there a way to get the benefit and change the metaprogram? For example, Carla's ability to think globally fits with her self-identity as a visionary and leader. She likes being able to capture her friends and family with her stories and ideas and finds the details boring. One way Carla can reduce resistance to this change is by finding value in developing ideas and sharing the information required to realize the global picture. Carla may find that reframing is a good strategy here.

Step 6: Check once more for resistance. Did reframing remove interference with the desired change?

Step 7: Adopt the change. Recall the four learning levels from Chapter 2. They are:

- **Subconscious incompetence:** You do not have the skill or even and awareness that the skill is needed.

- **Conscious incompetence:** You are aware that you do not yet have the skill, but there is a recognition that the skill is needed.

- **Conscious competence:** Your skill is emerging but not yet automatic.

- **Subconscious competence:** The skill has become such a natural part of your behavior that you can do it without thinking about it.

With time, you will become subconsciously competent with the new skill.

Understanding how you are motivated can improve outcomes and ultimately the ability to create success in your life. Think of the ways that you are "automatic." Are you generally negative? Are you always closing yourself off? Are you so extroverted and social that you don't get anything done? Think of yourself almost like software and begin to explore. By practicing the above exercise and staying dedicated, you'll eventually find things running smoother than you could have ever hoped for.

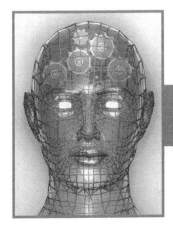

Anchoring

Have you ever known someone who said they got angry because they just couldn't help it? Sometimes it does feel like our emotions and feelings are in charge and we are helpless to stop them from taking over. Young adulthood is full of unexpected changes, and a lot of difficult emotions will arise with the new and important developments in your life. NLP offers a way to access a more resourceful state when you are dealing with challenging feelings. You can access or return to a more useful state by *anchoring*. Just as it sounds, this process will serve as the anchor for your ship in a tumultuous sea.

Anchors and Future Pacing

Anchors are one of the most powerful tools of NLP. Anchors provide immediate access to the most useful and appropriate state for the moment. Future pacing allows anchor users to practice being in that useful state so that it feels familiar. The following section includes a discussion of anchors and future pacing and how to use both.

Positive anchors

Positive anchors work by associating a stimulus — such as an action, sound, or symbol — with a desired state. The symbol or action becomes the stimulus for moving into the desired state. In other words, the symbol or action leads to the state in much the same way that flipping a switch leads to a light-filled room.

Here is another example: If you feel relaxed every time you hear jazz music, the music and the feeling of being relaxed become associated. Jazz music serves as the anchor for the state of relaxation. Choosing to turn on the music is referred to in NLP as "firing the anchor." If you begin to feel relaxed after you fire the anchor, you are said to have triggered the state.

In the beginning you may turn on, let's say, Charlie Parker because you heard from a friend that he or she finds the music soothing and relaxing. They love to listen to it just before sitting down to study. Or maybe you heard your parents playing his music while you drifted off to sleep one evening. At this stage, you are consciously aware of your desire to move into a relaxed state. With time, as the association between Charlie Parker and feeling relaxed grows stronger, you will find that your subconscious mind takes over.

Each time you hear the music, any tension you feel in your body will melt away, your breathing will probably slow, and feelings of stress will begin to fade. The state of relaxation will begin to fill you automatically with no conscious thought required.

You can use any anchor that you feel comfortable with. In fact, you probably already have experience with several anchors that you have never even thought about before. Do you and your friends love to listen to one particular song? Think about how you feel each time you hear the song. Without you even realizing it, the song has likely become an anchor for a state such as joy or excitement. Or think of the emotional and physical response you have each time you smell a pie baking or Thanksgiving dinner on the stove. The stimuli — the smell of the food — becomes the anchor, which evokes a predictable physical or emotional response. In the case of Thanksgiving dinner or pie baking, even the memory can trigger feelings of warmth, family, comfort, and celebration.

The key for establishing a positive anchor is to create a strong association between the desired state and the stimulus or the anchor. In this way, you trigger the state or reach the desired state automatically, without even thinking about it. Once the association has been set, the desired state follows.

There are many instances in our daily lives when we respond to both conscious and subconscious anchors. Ideally, we can set up anchors that help to achieve excellence, regardless of the setting. The best way to do this is to determine what state would be most useful in a particular situation. Consider the following:

What would be the best state to be in for:

- An interview for a competitive college
- Delivering a presentation
- School performance
- A regular school day
- Running a marathon
- Responding to an angry or upset parent or teacher

You are more likely to be your best self or in your most resourceful state when you take the time to understand what resources the circumstance will require. We will discuss more on how to do this later in the chapter.

Negative anchors

Since we understand the value of being able to get into the most resourceful state for any given circumstance, it is useful to be aware of how we respond to the different stimuli out there. When an anchor triggers a state that is not good for us, it is a negative anchor.

Sometimes the anchor or stimulus triggers an undesirable state. For example, there may be a certain person at school who you know is spreading rumors about you, and every time you see them, you start to sulk. Here's another more extreme but illustrative example: combat veterans often speak of the extreme anxiety they experience each time they hear loud noise or noises that remind them of gunfire. During combat, it was useful to be anxious and alert upon hearing loud or potentially dangerous noises. Outside the context of combat, that response is not necessarily useful. Thus, the stimulus of loud noise is a negative anchor. This example is more telling than any — negative anchors are usually not helpful. Sometimes, they take us out of the actual situation at hand and prevent us from acting effectively.

Anchors can create immense feelings of discomfort. Sometimes, these kinds of anchors can be used to manage behavior. If you've ever been the only kid in class not to finish an important assignment, you surely remember the look of disappointment and shock on your teacher's face. Maybe you were breaking up with a girlfriend or boyfriend and the sound of your phone ringing or phone buzzing gave you feelings of anxiety, heartbreak, or regret. And although they are uncomfortable, they can be incredibly instructive and helpful in the long term. Just think about all the messages we hear about cigarette smoking — by now, you must have some negative anchor associated with it, which is for the best. This negative anchor is protecting your long-term health and happiness — not to mention your breath!.

Yet, just as anchors are created, they can be broken. The process of breaking an anchor is called collapsing anchors, which will be discussed in the next chapter.

External stimuli that evoke an internal response

Anchors can be established with or without permission from your conscious mind. In our earlier example of the music, the anchor was likely set in your subconscious mind. You were not even aware that the anchor was being established. After all, you were likely just enjoying yourself instead of saying to yourself, "I am going to associate good feelings with this song, and every time I hear it I will experience feelings of love, romance, and happiness." The same is true of the pie baking. The experiences and feelings that become associated with the pie will become evident each time you smell the pie baking. It's not because you stopped and said aloud, "The wafting scent of this pie is inducing immense feelings of warmth and joy."

It can be helpful to think of an anchor as a conditioned response. The most well-known example of a conditioned response involves Pavlov, whom you may have already heard of. Born in 1849, Ivan Pavlov, a Russian psychologist, conducted several experiments during which he discovered that dogs would begin to salivate each time they encountered a stimulus they associated with food. Most famously, Pavlov's dogs are said to have salivated at the sound of a bell.

Less known is that Pavlov studied a number of stimuli. In fact, it is even documented that the dogs began to salivate when they saw lab technicians in their typical garb of white lab jackets. Because the lab technicians fed the dogs, they began to associate the techs with eating and would salivate just with the sight of them.

The example of Pavlov's dogs should make clear that virtually anything can become an anchor. The power of the anchor is not simply in the stimulus, it is in the close association between the stimulus and the experience. Like dogs, human beings respond.

Our experience of the environment is constantly imprinting on our memories and expectations. For example, most people are more likely to choose a package of chicken noodle soup that pictures a grandmotherly type proffering a steaming bowl of soup than they are to choose one labeled only with the words "chicken noodle soup." The package picturing the grandmother leads us to assume, either consciously or unconsciously, that that soup will be better because it is associated with grandma's soup lovingly made, or at least lovingly served. Even buyers who have not had such an experience of grandma serving them chicken noodle soup understand and are persuaded by the association.

The good news is we don't have to be passive and let the world create anchors for us. We can start taking control of our experience of the world by making associations for ourselves. We can associate studying with soothing music. Exercise with fresh air. Understanding anchors can help us plan external stimuli to evoke a particular desired response to achieve our goals and dreams.

Link a positive state to a past occasion and relive it to set it

If you have ever run a 5K or a marathon, delivered an excellent presentation, or successfully completed a project, then you are familiar with the resource state. A resource state is a positive, proactive, potential-filled experience. Future pacing allows you to connect resource states to cues in your future so that when needed, they can be triggered to help you achieve the best state for the circumstance.

Let's go back to the list created earlier. On the list were several scenarios for which it would be helpful to determine the most useful state in advance. We will now look at two of these scenarios — delivering a presentation and talking to an angry parent or teacher. When delivering a presentation, the most useful state would likely include feeling prepared, confident, and relaxed. If you are talking with a distressed authority figure, the best state might be feeling patient, reasonable, and humble. You can create these feelings or any feeling you need for any situation by linking to a positive state from a past occasion and reliving it to set it. NLP uses an acronym for the process of setting anchors. The easy-to-remember acronym is RACE, which will be outlined in the next chapter.

Now, you probably already have a set of ideas for what you might use as anchors. Before moving on to the next chapter, take out a pencil and notepad (because we know you've had it out this entire time!) and make a two-column list. Label one column "negative anchors" and the other "positive anchors." Try to think of five positive anchors you already have (smell of pie = warmth and family) and negative anchors (punk rock = anger and frustration). You will most likely want to change some of the ones you already have. The next chapter will show you to do just that.

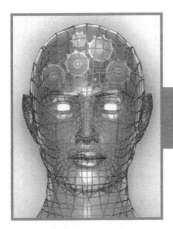

CHAPTER 9

Creating Positive Anchors and Using Them Effectively

L et's say you're delivering a presentation. Sound terrifying? Well, you're not alone. Public speaking is among the top five fears for most people, and the very idea causes them to break out in a cold sweat. Obviously, this is not the most useful state to achieve excellence in presentations. Remember that NLP mantra, *if anyone can do it then anyone can learn to do it*. RACE shows you how to create a positive anchor and enter your most useful state.

<u>R</u>elive — Perhaps you don't feel confident about public speaking yet. But you probably have experienced feelings of confidence in a different setting. The first step in setting an anchor is to relive or recall as vividly as possible an experience where you felt confident.

Go to a place where you are not likely to be distracted or interrupted; you will need several minutes to fully focus on the experience. As you recall the experience of feeling confident, use each of the submodalities. Remember those? Engaging the visual (sight), auditory (sound), kinesthetic (feeling), olfactory (smell), and gustatory (taste) submodalities can make the recall experience seem more vivid and real.

When recalling your experience, ask yourself: What did I see? Fine-tune your visual modality by making the colors as sharp and bright as you can. What did you hear, feel, smell, and taste? Again, turn the volume up on each of those sensory memories. Reliving is the closest thing we have to time travel or "do-overs." The internal experience of the event in memory should be created so vividly that it matches the physical experience in reality.

Reliving positive experiences allows you to harness the useful feelings produced to fuel additional excellent experiences. Maybe you don't really remember having an experience with the feeling you want to create. Well, you're in luck. Use the power of your imagination. You can still set the anchor by imagining that you had the experience. Even if the memory is not your own, you have likely experienced the feeling through a friend or even through a character in a book or movie.

Anchor. As you experience feeling confident, you must associate a stimulus or anchor with this state. Associating a stimulus or anchoring the state allows you to access and use the good feelings to create the same state whenever you need it.

Choose any anchor you like. Many successful anchors are set with different parts of the body — usually the hands — so that they are always accessible and ready to be fired. Folding the hands together is an anchor that has been previously mentioned in this book. Other body anchors

might include positioning or crossing the fingers in a certain way. The key is to choose an anchor that feels right for you and that you are likely to use. Choose one that plays to your strengths or your "primary representational mode."

Remember that the sense or representational modes are visual, auditory, kinesthetic, olfactory, and gustatory. If you consider yourself to be an auditory person, then an auditory anchor may be best for you. For example, as you fold your hands together you might also say something to yourself like, "I feel confident," or "delivering presentations is really easy for me."

Change or create a distraction. As soon as the anchor is set, seek out a distraction that takes you out of the state for which you have set the anchor. "Breaking state" can be as simple as changing your train of thought. Instead of reliving the experience you are using to set the anchor you can switch your thoughts to what you will have for dinner or your schedule for the next several days. The key is to remove yourself from the state that you are anchoring.

This is basically a way to "test" your anchor. You want to be able to create a state that has a *finite* end. The kind of confidence you want to build for public speaking may not be the kind of focus you want for reading an intensive textbook. You want to be able to break away from it, and create a sort of "packaged" feeling.

Evoke or test your anchor. After you have spent a few minutes doing your homework or filling in your planner (or whatever you've been doing), fold your hands to evoke feelings of confidence. See if you feel like you're entering a magical portal of some sort into your desired state of mind. If you do, then hurrah! You've successfully created your anchor.

If after you have gone through each of the steps you are unable to evoke the desired response, don't worry. Run through each of the steps again, giving particular attention to each of the modalities. You should be fully in the experience as if it is happening in the moment. Creating strong anchors is most successful when you set the anchor during the most intense part of the relived experience. You can repeat the four steps of creating an anchor with many different positive experiences to improve your chances of reliably evoking the desired response. In NLP, the process of repeating these steps with many positive experiences is known as "stacking anchors."

Resource — an anchor that genuinely provides good feelings

Remember the presupposition, "People have all the resources they need"? Anchors help you immediately access any internal resource you need in a given moment. Imagine being plagued by a feeling of anxiety. But anxiety is only one of the many feelings you have experienced in your life. You have also experienced calm and confidence. Anchoring allows you to access the feeling of calm if it is more appropriate than anxiety for the situation at hand.

Collapsing — a process for breaking negative anchors

Previously, we discussed negative anchors. An anchor or stimulus, whether it is positive or negative, generates a physiological response. Like positive anchors, negative anchors can be set during any experience that creates an association. When that response is not useful for where we are or what we are trying to accomplish, we can break the anchor. Breaking the anchor is also called collapsing the anchor. The following exercise includes the steps for collapsing anchors.

Exercise 9:
Collapsing Anchors

If a particular anchor evokes an unwanted state, NLP can help you remove that anchor and create a positive one that triggers a more useful state. Collapsing, neutralizing, or extinguishing anchors works by triggering opposing states (positive and negative) simultaneously. Ideally, the positive state, which is stronger, wins over the negative state — neutralizing it.

Step 1: Determine which state you want to break. For example, if every time you hear the word "jump" you feel afraid, the state you want to break is fear. You want to break the association between hearing the word jump and your response of fear that the word elicits.

Step 2: Decide how you want to feel instead. For example, you may decide that each time you hear the word jump, you want to feel relaxed or happy instead of fear.

Step 3: Create a positive anchor using the steps learned with RACE. Relive the positive experience associated with the way you want to feel when you hear the word jump. Anchor the feeling using one or more stimuli such as a hand position and a word or phrase you say to yourself. Change your thoughts; break the state by allowing your mind to be occupied by a completely different train of thought. Evoke the desired feeling by firing the anchor or anchors you have chosen to trigger the state.

Step 4: It is important that you remember to break state after you create the anchor for the positive feelings you want to trigger. After you break state, you will then create an anchor for the negative state, again using the steps learned with RACE. Also, remember to test your anchor to be sure that it evokes the desired response. In this case, you should have two anchors for two responses: the feeling you want to have (relaxed or happy) and the feeling you do not want to have (fear).

Step 5: Break state again by distracting yourself with unrelated thoughts such as who won last week's ballgame or what *Apple* will come up with next.

Step 6: Fire both the positive and the negative anchors in succession. Do not break state between firing the opposing anchors. After two or three rounds, fire both anchors simultaneously. Break the anchor associated with the negative state while maintaining the anchor associated with the positive state.

Step 7: Test again by firing the negative anchor. If you have collapsed the anchor, you will not evoke the fear response or maybe what you experience will be a reduced fear response. You may even feel no response and feel completely neutral in response to the anchor that was previously associated with fear. If you are still experiencing unwanted feelings, you can repeat the RACE steps or combine anchors. For example, pair a hand position (crossed fingers) with a word (carefree), or a word with a sound (water), or an object (a smooth stone you hold) with a word.

Using Anchors Effectively

There are three important points to remember about anchors:

1. The anchor should be set right at or just a few seconds before the most intense or peak portion of the recall experience. For example, if you are anchoring confidence to finish a race, you would begin by reliving another race that you completed successfully. Set your anchor just before you cross the finish line and hold it until just after you cross the finish line in your mind. By doing this, you capture the most intense feelings with which you will associate your anchor. Remember to interrupt or break state just after you cross the finish line so you anchor only the wanted feeling — confidence to finish the race and not an unintended feeling, such as tired or worried about an injury after the race.

2. The anchor should be unique. Avoid an anchor that you commonly use. For example, if your anchor is crossed fingers, be sure that you only use crossed fingers to trigger that state and not under other circumstances.

3. Finally, your anchor should be consistent so that it is firmly and reliably established. Every time you want to trigger the state of confidence in races, fire the trigger in exactly the same way.

As we discussed earlier, anchors can be established consciously or subconsciously. Anchors can also be set by individuals and with others. To use anchors most effectively, it is important to understand how you respond to the many types of stimuli you experience. How you experience stimuli often depends on the strength of the association and, in some cases, the setting in which the stimuli is present. For example, how you respond to a certain stimulus at a party might be different from the way you would respond at school. Using anchors effectively requires some knowledge of how and when you respond to stimuli and knowing when a response should be encouraged or extinguished.

Using the TOTE model to check your progress

The TOTE model — Test, Operate, Test, Exit — is a basic strategy for checking progress with anything you are doing. For example, you can use the TOTE model to test the association between your anchor and desired state, and you can use it to check if you have successfully set an anchor or created rapport with another person. TOTE works like this: Test to be sure you are getting the result you want, operate or tweak what you are doing if you are not getting the results you want, test again to see if you are now getting the results you want, and exit when you get the result you want or when you decide to stop trying for the result.

When setting an anchor, it can be useful to gauge the intensity of the feeling that you trigger on a scale of one to 10, with 10 being the most intense. Successful anchors trigger the most intense feelings. If your anchor does not consistently trigger the intended resource state, avoid firing it. If you fire an anchor that should trigger confidence and it triggers anxiety instead, it is self-defeating.

Altering states with anchors

Anchors help us organize our internal resources against the external stimuli. If at any time external stimuli trigger a negative state, it is possible to alter that state with anchors. Altering states helps us access the resources that are needed for the situation at hand.

Altering your state is much like changing the direction of a car you're driving. For example, let's say you are driving down the road one day. When you come to a stop light, a car next to you says that your tire looks flat. Instead of continuing on your way, you turn into a garage on the corner. You had a problem, and rather than continue driving on a soon to be flat tire, you immediately accessed the readily available resource of the garage to move out of the problem state (your flat tire) and into a desired state (good tire).

Here's how altering states might look in your external and internal world. You have heard that you are not the most patient person around. You gather this feedback is accurate because your friends, parents, or teachers have told you. Being patient has become particularly important lately because it is the foundation of your plan to improve your academic life. You have set an auditory anchor (the word *calm*) and a visual anchor (ocean waves). Because you understand that it is within your power to control what you think, how you feel, and what you do, you decide that each time you find yourself approaching the unwanted state (impatience), you will fire your anchors. In that way, you come to have control of yourself based on what happens within you, rather than what happens around you.

Anchors are a powerful way to employ our best resources in service to our goal of excellence. It doesn't matter what problem state you are trying to change into a desired state; the change is always possible. Improve your chances of success by using as many of your sense modes as you can while reliving your positive experiences. Set your anchor at the peak of the relived experience. Consider using multiple anchors, such as pairing an auditory and visual anchor. Remember that stacking several positive experiences on the same anchor can strengthen the anchor.

Anchors help us exercise control over our thoughts and feelings. Anchors also eliminate the paralysis and loss of control that often results from negative thoughts and feelings. Use anchors to access any resourceful feeling you might need in certain circumstance. Even if you have never experienced the feeling, the ability to create an anchor is still available to you. Simply use an experience that you read or heard about. You will quickly find that many of the roadblocks in your life that seemed insurmountable will begin to shrink. This is because, as you know, people have all the resources they need.

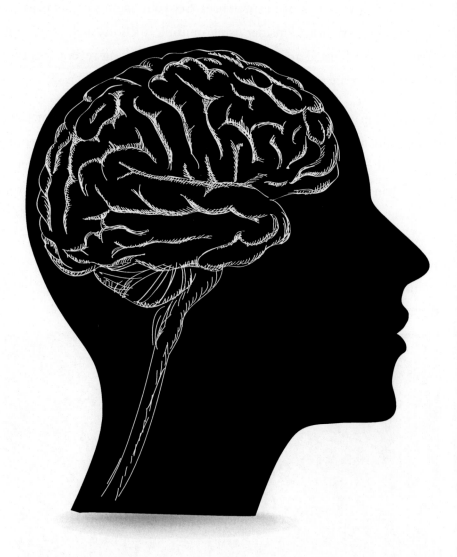

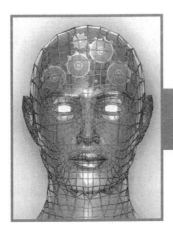

NLP is a valuable tool for achieving excellence in your own life. Use NLP to break through limiting beliefs, eliminate phobias, achieve desired outcomes, and operate from your most useful state. There are no limits to what you can do with NLP when you practice and apply the patterns and strategies.

There is much to learn with NLP, or neuro-linguistic programming. The most important things to remember about these revolutionary strategies, presuppositions, and patterns are:

- **If a thing has been done, it can be done.** Remember that, at its core, NLP is about modeling human excellence. If you are struggling with anything at all, know that you can end the struggle by understanding how someone who was struggling with your problem found success. If someone is experiencing more success than you are with anything, it is probably because he or she is bringing different resources to the task or using the same resources differently. Even if you do not feel like you have immediate access to the required resources, remember that you do. People have all the resources they need.

- **You always have immediate access to your desired state.** Remember the power of anchoring to shift a non-useful state to a useful one.

- **You can change your mind and your behavior with NLP.** It does not matter how long you have had a behavior or a thought. You can create new thoughts, feelings, and behaviors with NLP.

In the next section, you will find many of the key ideas from this book. Refer to these often as you work to change your mind and your behavior.

NLP for Successful Communication

These pillars are the basis for the NLP philosophy, and all NLP concepts are supported by these pillars.

Behavioral flexibility

As the word flexibility suggests, this pillar is concerned with one's ability to adapt his or her actions as a strategy for influencing a particular response from, and in response to, another person.

Sensory acuity

Paying attention to small changes in facial expression or eye movement helps us determine if what we are saying resonates with or annoys others. It is important to note here that body language is as unique as individuals themselves.

Rapport

The goal in creating rapport is not wholesale agreement of everything that is being communicated, but rather to show the other person that you understand what they are trying to communicate.

There are three output channels: words, voice, and body. To get a full understanding of what is being communicated, you must survey, interpret, and respond to all three output channels.

Outcome thinking

Outcome thinking encourages us to clearly define what we want so we are more likely to get it. Outcome thinking helps us shift from the problem to the process of considering solutions.

These four pillars of NLP are the building blocks for successful communication. Use them to your advantage, keep practicing, and enjoy the fruits of your hard-earned work!

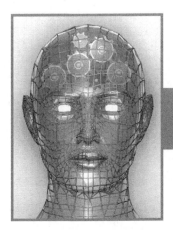

Anchoring: Connects an internal response with an external trigger. Anchors can be visual, auditory, kinesthetic, olfactory, or gustatory.

Associated: Having a remembered experience from the first person perceptual position. In connecting with the experience through your own sense modes, you see, hear, and feel what is happening while it happens.

Auditory: Concerned with hearing; one of the sense modes.

Away from: A type of metaprogram where the preference of the person is to move away from a punishment. The opposite of the "away from" motivation is a "toward" motivation.

Break state: Interruption of your current emotional state.

Chunking: Gathering pieces of information into smaller or larger groups or pieces. Chunking up organizes pieces of information into larger groups, while chunking down moves information into smaller groups.

Congruence: Finding agreement among all the internal behaviors, thoughts, feelings, and beliefs.

Deep structure: The inherent or implied, but unexpressed, meaning in language.

Deletion: Expressed language that does not include deep structure. In other words, the details have not been included leaving the listener to make assumptions about what has been said.

Dissociated: Having a remembered experience from the third person perceptual position. In other words, not connecting with the experience, but seeing it as an observer.

Distortion: Using language to present an inaccurate picture or description of an event.

Ecology: The larger system in which individuals function. NLP advocates looking at the entire life (for example, work, place of faith, family, friends) to see if changes can be supported or if they will be undermined by unintended consequences or outcomes.

Elicitation: Involves using questions to understand internal processing.

Eye accessing cues: Eye movement patterns that reveal how a person is processing information or what they are thinking and feeling.

Generalization: Extending a unique or specific experience into a model for every similar group of experiences.

Gustatory: Concerned with taste; one of the sense modes.

Internal representation: Individual patterns of storing memories, thoughts and ideas, and experiences using each of the sense modes.

Kinesthetic: Concerned with feeling (both tactile and emotional); one of the sense modes.

Matching: Copying the behavior patterns of another person to create rapport.

Meta model: One of the first two models developed by NLP co-founders Grinder and Bandler, meta models gather information into smaller chunks to improve communication by removing generalizations, distortions, and deletions.

Milton model: Named for noted hypnotherapist Milton Erikson, this model chunks up details to allow the listener to access the subconscious in search of information.

Mirroring: Adopting some of the behavior patterns of another person to build rapport.

Modeling: Copying the successful behavior of others to achieve success in your own life.

Olfactory: Concerned with smelling; one of the sense modes.

Pacing: Establishing rapport with matching some of the behaviors, such as voice tone. Pacing ends with leading. Here is an example of the pattern: pace, pace, pace, lead.

Perceptual position: One of the points of view from which to regard a situation. The positions are first (yourself), second (the listener), and third (an observer).

Predicates: Words that reveal which representational system the speaker is using. For example, "I see" would suggest a visual representational system.

Presupposition: A statement with an underlying meaning that is assumed to be true.

Rapport: The process of building meaningful connection with another person.

Representational systems: Related to the sense modes that are used to represent experiences, memories, and ideas internally.

Resources: A broad term used to include all the things used to achieve a desired outcome. Examples of resources include beliefs, language, and emotional states.

State: How a person is thinking and feeling at a given moment.

Submodalities: Distinctions that allow for fine-tuning the sense modes. For example, in the visual submodality, there is the ability to brighten, darken, or remove color from an internal representation.

Visual: Concerned with sight; one of the sense modes.

Well-formed outcome: The formula for achieving a desired outcome, which says it must be stated in the positive, self-controlled, right sized, and ecological.

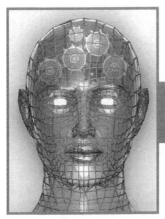

BIBLIOGRAPHY

Andreas, Steve, and Charles Faulkner, eds. *NLP: The New Technology of Achievement*. New York: Harper Collins, 1994.

Beever, Sue. *Happy Kids, Happy You: Using NLP to Bring Out the Best in Ourselves and the Children We Care For*. Wales: Crown Publishing, 2009.

Culbert, Samuel, and Lawrence Rout. *Get Rid of the Performance review: How Companies Can Stop Intimidating and Start Managing*. New York: Business Plus, 2010.

Galatiltyte, Rasa. *Beyond Rapid Therapy: Modern NLP Concepts & Methods*. Inner Patch Publishing 2009

Terry, Roger, and Richard Churches. *NLP for Teacher: How to Be a Highly Effective Teacher*. Wales: Crown House Publishing, 2008.

Terry, Roger, and Richard Churches. *The NLP Toolkit for Teachers, Trainers and School Leaders*. Wales: Crown House Publishing, 2009.

Vaknin, Shlomo. *NLP for Beginners: Only the Essentials*. Inner Patch Publishing, 2009.

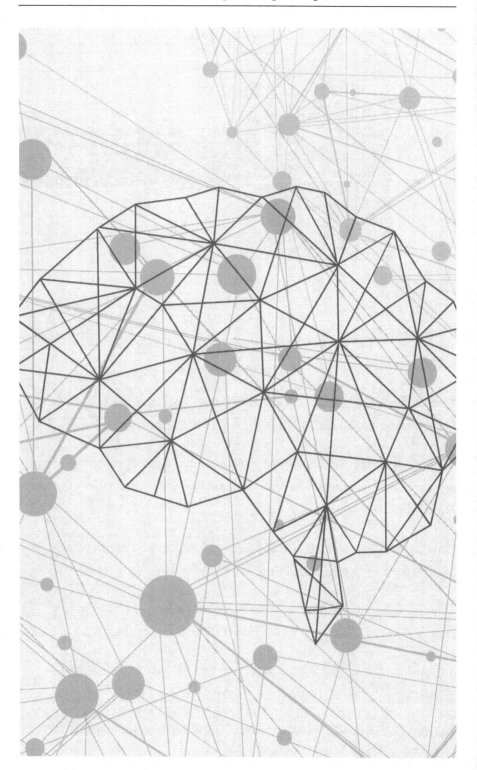

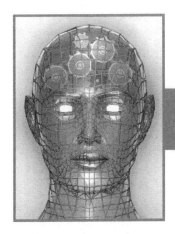

INDEX